The Man, His Mission
and His Message

Introducing

Paul

Michael F. Bird

IVP Academic
An imprint of InterVarsity Press
Downers Grove, Illinois

InterVarsity Press
P.O. Box 1400, Downers Grove, IL 60515-1426
Internet: www.ivpress.com
E-mail: email@ivpress.com

©Michael F. Bird, 2008

Published in the United States of America by InterVarsity Press, Downers Grove, Illinois, with permission from Inter-Varsity Press, England.

InterVarsity Press® is the book-publishing division of InterVarsity Christian Fellowship/USA®, a student movement active on campus at hundreds of universities, colleges and schools of nursing in the United States of America, and a member movement of the International Fellowship of Evangelical Students. For information about local and regional activities, write Public Relations Dept., InterVarsity Christian Fellowship/USA, 6400 Schroeder Rd., P.O. Box 7895, Madison, WI 53707-7895, or visit the IVCF website at <www.intervarsity.org>.

Scripture quotations marked NET are from The NET Bible, New English Translation. Copyright *©1996-2003 by Biblical Studies Press LLC. All rights reserved.*

ISBN 978-0-8308-2897-5

Printed in the United States of America ∞

 InterVarsity Press is committed to protecting the environment and to the responsible use of natural resources. As a member of Green Press Initiative we use recycled paper whenever possible. To learn more about the Green Press Initiative, visit <www.greenpressinitiative.org>.

Library of Congress Cataloging-in-Publication Data
A catalog record for this book is available from the Library of Congress.

P	16	15	14	13	12	11	10	9	8	7	6	5	4	3	2	1
Y	22	21	20	19	18	17	16	15	14	13	12	11	10	09		

CONTENTS

PREFACE

This book is meant as an introduction to the apostle Paul for laypersons and undergraduate students and as a refresher for pastors and ministers. My objective is to get people excited about reading Paul's letters, preaching Paul's gospel and living the Christian life the way Paul thought it should be lived. My aim is to go deeper into Paul but without losing people in the mire of scholarly debates and complex technicalities. I want to show that what Paul has to say to the church today is both relevant and riveting.

I have an endless list of people to whom I owe a debt of gratitude. First, I must thank Scot McKnight (North Park University) for encouraging me to write something at a more popular and accessible level about Paul. Scot himself is a great example of how biblical scholarship should be done in service to the church and in order to make the Bible come alive for Christians. I also have to thank Phil Duce (IVP-UK) for supporting this project from the beginning. My wife Naomi and daughters Alexis and Alyssa are never far from my mind when I write on this and they have shared the journey with me from the beginning. My dear Naomi has had to listen to the same sermons on Paul countless times and deserves a medal for enduring them. The students of my Romans and Pauline theology classes at the Highland Theological College deserve a vote of thanks for putting up with my ravings in lectures and my constant references to ideas cooking in my mind. The folk at Dingwall Baptist Church endured many of my ideas formulated here in sermons and Bible studies and I hope that their faith is richer for the experience. My colleagues at Highland Theological

College also earn my thanks for providing advice and encouragement during the writing of this book. They embody the virtues of
humanitas and *caritas* and make my work a labour of love. My
thanks also to several persons who read chapters of this book and
offered comment, including Michael Gorman, Michael Pahl,
Hector Morrison, Jason Hood, Heather Robins, Joshua Schow,
Debbie Hunn and Richard Myerscough.

Finally, I dedicate this book to my in-laws, Stewart and Helen
Lanyon, who have treated me like a son, as well as Timothy,
Courtney and (yes, even) Sarah, who have loved me like a brother.
Thanks for providing me with a beautiful and godly wife! I also
hope that this gesture will placate the wrath of my mother-in-law,
who, I suspect, wishes to have me 'taken care of' because I took
her eldest daughter and all of her grandchildren to Scotland from
Australia and now another daughter wants to emigrate to Scotland
after visiting here. But should that hitman one day come for me
and beat me to death with a very sharp pineapple, at least I can say,
'I know whom I have believed in and I am persuaded that he is
able to protect what has been entrusted to me until that day'
(2 Tim. 2:12).

Michael F. Bird

Soli Deo Gloria

ABBREVIATIONS

1 Macc.	1 Maccabees
2 Macc.	2 Maccabees
4 Macc.	4 Maccabees
1QS	*Rule of the Community*
2 Bar.	*2 Baruch*
1 Clem.	*Clement of Rome, 1 Clement*
4Q521	*Messiah of Heaven and Earth*
11QtgJob	*Targum of Job*
ACCS	Ancient Christian Commentary on Scripture
Abr.	*De Abrahamo* (Philo)
ABRL	Anchor Bible Reference Library
Ant.	*Jewish Antiquities* (Josephus)
ANTC	Abingdon New Testament Commentaries
Apoc. Ab.	*Apocalypse of Abraham*
AUC	*Ab urbe condita* (Livy)
AV	Authorized (King James) Version
Bar.	Baruch
BBR	*Bulletin for Biblical Research*
BDAG	W. Bauer, W. F. Arndt, F. W. Danker and W. F. Gingrich, *A Greek–English Lexicon of the New Testament and Other Early Christian Literature*, 3rd ed. (Chicago: University of Chicago Press, 2000)
b. Šab.	*Babylonian Talmud, Šabbat*
BZNW	Beihefte zur Zeitschrift für die Neutestamentliche Wissenschaft
CBQ	*Catholic Biblical Quarterly*

Cels.	*Contra Celsum* (Origen)
Claud.	*Divus Claudius* (Suetonius)
Did.	*Didache*
DNTB	*Dictionary of New Testament Background* (Downers Grove, IL: IVP; Leicester: IVP, 2000)
DPL	*Dictionary of Paul and His Letters* (Downers Grove, IL: IVP; Leicester: IVP, 1993)
Ec.	*Eclogues* (Virgil)
Ep.	*Epistle* (Philostratus)
EQ	Evangelical Quarterly
ESV	English Standard Version
Eth. nic.	*Ethica nicomachea* (Aristotle)
FS	Festschrift
Gen. Rab.	*Genesis Rabbah*
Hist.	*Histories* (Tacitus)
Gos. Truth	*Gospel of Truth*
Hist. eccl.	*Historia ecclesiastica* (Eusebius)
ICC	International Critical Commentary
Interp	Interpretation Commentary Series
JB	Jerusalem Bible
JSNT	*Journal for the Study of the New Testament*
JTS	*Journal of Theological Studies*
Jub.	*Jubilees*
LAB	*Liber antiquitatum biblicarum*
LAE	*Life of Adam and Eve*
LANE	A. Deissmann, *Light from the Ancient Near East*, trans. L. R. M. Strachan (Peabody: Hendrickson, 1995)
Macc.	Maccabees
Mart. Pol.	*Martyrdom of Polycarp*
NAB	New American Bible
NASB	New American Standard Bible
NCB	New Century Bible
NCBC	New Cambridge Bible Commentary
NET	New English Translation
NICNT	New International Commentary on the New Testament
NIGTC	New International Greek Testament Commentary

NIV	New International Version
NIVAC	New International Version Application Commentary
NKJV	New King James Version
NRSV	New Revised Standard Version
NSBT	New Studies in Biblical Theology
PBM	Paternoster Biblical Monographs
Pel.	*Pelopidas* (Plutarch)
P.Oxy	Papyrus Oxyrhynchus
Pr. Azar.	Prayer of Azariah
Pss. Sol.	*Psalms of Solomon*
RSV	Revised Standard Version
SBET	*Scottish Bulletin of Evangelical Theology*
SCS	Septuagint Commentary Series
Sib. Or.	*Sybilline Oracles*
Sifra	*Sifra* (Midrash on Leviticus)
Sir.	Sirach
SJT	*Scottish Journal of Theology*
Symp.	*Symposium* (Plato)
T. Benj.	*Testament of Benjamin*
T. Levi	*Testament of Levi*
T. Mos.	*Testament of Moses*
Tusc.	*Tusculanae disputationes* (Cicero)
TynBul	*Tyndale Bulletin*
War	*Jewish War* (Josephus)
WBC	Word Biblical Commentary

1. WHAT IS PAUL?

'What is Paul?' This is the question Paul rhetorically posed to the Corinthians when he learned that factions were emerging in Corinth, factions centred around individuals like himself and Apollos (1 Cor. 1:10–17; 3:4–5). What is Paul, then? In his own words, he is a 'servant' through whom the message of the gospel rings out. A similar designation occurs at the beginning of many of Paul's letters; for example, Romans: 'Paul, a servant of Jesus Christ' (Rom. 1:1).[1] Paul defines his ministry and identity as that of a bond-slave of Jesus Christ with a resolute commitment to the call and cause of the gospel. To venerate Paul is to denigrate the Saviour whom he so passionately serves. Paul does not let himself become the centre of a personality cult. He puts his ministry in the context of planting and watering and points out that it is ultimately God who makes things grow, so it is God who must receive the glory (1 Cor. 3:5–10).

We can change the question slightly from 'What is Paul?' to

---

1. Unless stated otherwise, all Bible translations are my own.

'*Who* is Paul?' Part of the problem in answering that question is that we have a contemptible familiarity with him. Yes, we all know Paul, don't we? He was the apostle to the Gentiles, witness of the exalted Christ, preacher of the gospel, the great theologian of the church and author of many epistles. On any given week, Christians read over Paul in their daily devotions in want of spiritual nourishment, preachers crawl through his letters in search of inspiration, theologians wrestle with the profundity of his thinking, and talk shows inevitably have something to say about his view of women and homosexuality.

Paul is our theological master, our pastoral mentor, our spiritual adviser and our missionary hero. Paul is the Christian who has become all things to all people. Yet just when we think we have him in our grasp, we find he slips through our fingers. At the point where we suppose we have finally understood him, he again confounds us and stirs our hearts and minds further. Just when we think we have wrestled with Paul and triumphed, we find him sitting on top of us with our faces in the dust. Alas, trying to nail him down can be like attempting to nail jelly to a wall. Paul, the great apostle, defies our caricatures of him; he deconstructs our neat little theological systems; he repels any attempt to put him in a corner and make him sit still: he remains the elusive apostle.

So how well do we really know him? If the Paul we claim to know looks and sounds a lot like us, then that is probably a good indication that we do not know him as well as we think we do. There is always a temptation to recruit him to our cause, to make our enemies his enemies, our beliefs his beliefs. Plus, our information about him is scant and fragmentary. Paul left us neither a travel diary nor a systematic theology textbook to follow. At the end of the day, we have only a 'Reader's Digest' account of his life from Luke (in the Acts of the Apostles) and some thirteen pastoral postcards he sent to the churches of his day. What is more, Paul remains historically and culturally distant from our time, for he inhabited a world utterly foreign to our own. Notwithstanding our dangerous familiarity with Paul and the temptation to make him out to be one of us, the limited sources at our disposal and our physical distance from him should put us on guard before claiming too much about him.

However, all is not lost. If we can be mature enough to let Paul be Paul and treat his letters as windows into his world rather than as deposits of theological dogma, then we stand a chance of meeting him anew, letting him speak for himself in his language, on his terms and for his purposes. Our search is not for a disembodied mind lurking beneath two-thousand-year-old texts. Instead, our quest is for a teacher who has something he wants to tell us, if only we have ears to hear and hearts ready to obey.

So, why study Paul in the first place? For a start, Paul was the towering force behind much of early Christianity. No other follower of Jesus shaped the early Christian movement in the first two centuries as much as Paul did. The writings attributed to him take up 24% of the New Testament. Paul has been canonized as a saint, has had cathedrals named in his honour, has been the subject of television documentaries. Musicians set his words to music, churches divide over what they think he meant, massive tomes are regularly written about him, and stained-glass windows bear the image of the man whose face no one would recognize even if they saw it. What is more, in the history of the Christian church, times of reformation and renewal have often found their catalyst in fresh encounters with the apostle. Paul, the servant of Jesus Christ, has a fresh word from God for the church in all ages. It is by understanding Paul that we better understand the Lord he served, and through Paul we can discover new depths to Christ's glory and new heights to God's magnificence.

Paul is known best through his epistles, which is where he truly comes alive to us.[2] He wrote letters for a variety of reasons: to encourage and rebuke congregations, to exhort individuals in their ministry, to defend his authority and ministry and to establish fellowship with Christians he did not know personally. Paul writes as a substitute for his personal presence and to convey his viewpoint in troubling situations. In divine providence, these letters were written *for us*, but were not originally written *to us*. All of Paul's letters are occasional in that they are written to specific churches or individuals in specific circumstances. At times Paul requests that his letters

---

2. N. A. Dahl, *Studies in Paul* (Minneapolis: Augsburg, 1977), p. 6.

be read widely and be given to other churches as well (e.g. 1 Thess. 5:27; Col. 4:16), showing he has an eye on the utility and value of his letters for addressing other churches too. Possibly one or two of Paul's letters, particularly Ephesians, were circular letters and were designed for widespread circulation. Those after Paul who collected his many letters and bound them into one compilation did so because they believed his words were inspired by God and of great relevance to Christians even after Paul's time. That is unsurprising, since Paul's letters are simultaneously theological, missional and pastoral. His letters continued to be of relevance to Christians in environs altogether different from those of their original recipients.

The issues Paul deals with (divorce, how to live a God-pleasing life, confronting aberrant doctrines, fund-raising, fostering unity etc.) are applicable to our day as much as to his time. Paul writes for the people of God, for their edification and encouragement. The effective history of Paul's literary endeavours is that he writes for the church local and universal, whether in Corinth or Chicago, Ephesus or London, Philippi or Sydney, the first century or the twenty-first century. He writes for the people of God in all ages and in all places so they can attain the full measure of maturity in Christ.

Paul is worth listening to not merely because he is an apostle and witness to Christ, nor simply for the fact that his letters are canonized as Scripture. Rather, it is because he has the heart of a pastor and his letters are concerned with helping and encouraging Christians in their corporate life. The people of God have much to learn from Paul about what it means to follow Jesus in a post-Christian, postmodern and pluralistic world: in short, a world becoming more and more conformed to the ancient world of Paul.

If you want to know what it means to follow Jesus in a world with gay marriages, where military threats loom in the Middle East, where different Jesuses are preached on television, where Christians are denounced for failing to embrace religious diversity, where some Christians even accommodate their faith to postmodernity, where Christians look more like the world than Christ, and where keeping Christians of varied convictions together in worshipful unity is increasingly difficult, then Paul is the author you need to read, since his experience is similar to yours.

If you are sick of spiritual 'milk' and crave 'meat', if you want to have a faith that is simultaneously thoughtful and pastoral, if you want to know the big picture but don't want to skimp on the details, then Paul is the author you need to read, for he is the one who most in the New Testament combines pastoral insights with profound theological reflection. A fresh encounter with Paul will leave your assumptions shaken to their foundations, your theological world turned upside down, your spirituality revitalized, your faith quickened, your love for God and Christ renewed, and your labour in the kingdom refocused. This is Paul for the people of God.

To uncover the mystery of Paul, I intend to cover a lot of territory and look at various aspects of his life, ministry and theology and the significance they hold for us today. But before we get down to business, a good way to get a basic grip on his career and thought is to look at five images of Paul reflected in the New Testament: *persecutor*, *missionary*, *theologian*, *pastor* and *martyr*.

Persecutor

At one point in Galatians, Paul recounts elements of his life prior to his conversion and reports, 'You have heard of my former way of life in Judaism. How intensely I was persecuting the church of God and was trying to destroy it' (Gal. 1:13). In Philippians, he states that the extent of his zeal in Judaism went as far as being 'a persecutor of the church' (Phil. 3:6). Paul considers himself the least of all the apostles because he previously persecuted the church (1 Cor. 15:9). He was once a militant Pharisee (Phil. 3:5; Acts 23:6; 26:5) and was committed to the law of Moses, to the purity of Israel and to an apocalyptic world view where the salvation of the present evil age would come directly from God. In Acts, Paul (or Saul as he was then known) was party to the public stoning of Stephen by an angry mob (Acts 7:58; 8:1) and 'voted' for the death of other Messiah followers (Acts 26:10).

Afterwards, Saul was 'ravaging the church, and entering house after house, he delivered over men and women and he put them in prison' (Acts 8:3). His determination to eradicate this deviant sect from the landscape led him even to go to the high priest and ask 'for letters to the synagogues at Damascus, so that if he found any who belonged to the Way, men or women, he might bind them and bring them to Jerusalem' (Acts 9:1–2). Saul of Tarsus, the cosmopolitan Jew learned in Greek and trained in Pharisaic lore, was pious in his religious faith and zealous in his commitment to protect Israel from apostasy and impurity. He was thoroughly devoted to the traditions of the fathers as the way of righteousness for the nation. Like many religious men of his day and ours, Saul believed his actions were in the name of God and were for the good of others. So it is true that the most heinous acts of violence are not committed by men who believe that what they do is malevolent, but rather are done by those who believe that what they do is righteous.

Given Saul's lust for the destruction of the disciples, his relentless persecution of believers and his willingness to travel to regions beyond Judea to seize followers of Jesus, it is no wonder that reports of his conversion were met with suspicion (Acts 9:26–27). When the genuineness of Paul's conversion became apparent, it was equally unsurprising that, as he narrates, the churches of Judea 'glorified God because of me' (Gal. 1:24). And what glory Paul brought to Christ as well!

We shall look at Paul's conversion and call later. Suffice it to say that we shall never understand him unless we come to terms with the radical transformation that occurred in his person, which turned him from persecutor into proclaimer. It is this radical revelation of God's grace that leads Paul to regard his inherited privileges and personal achievements as *skybala*, or what I translate as 'human filth' (Phil. 3:8). It is human filth compared to Christ, in whom Paul says he has gained a better righteousness than that under the law, and through Christ alone he hopes to attain the resurrection from the dead (Phil. 3:6–11). In his letters, Paul often contrasts the current life and status of Christians in Christ with their former way of life and status apart from Christ (e.g. 1 Cor. 1:26–31; 6:9–11; 12:2; Gal. 4:8–9; Eph. 2:1–3; Col. 1:21; 3:7). Paul applies that to himself as well, as is evident from Galatians 1 and

Philippians 3. Elsewhere in the Pastoral Epistles we read, 'But I was shown mercy so that in me, the quintessential sinner, Christ Jesus might display his unlimited patience as an example for those who would believe on him and receive eternal life' (1 Tim. 1:16). It was grace as an event, not merely a doctrine, that made this sinner and persecutor of the body of Christ a 'herald and an apostle' (1 Tim. 2:7).

Missionary

One of the most significant events of the Second World War was Hitler's decision to switch the focus of the German army from western Europe (and the invasion of Great Britain) to eastern Europe in order to commence the invasion of Russia in 1940. Historians believe it was this decision that cost Hitler the war. Likewise, in the history of Christian missions, one of the most significant turning points was Paul's decision to shift his attention from the east and to head west. After his conversion, Paul spent his initial years in Damascus and Arabia (Acts 9:20–25; 2 Cor. 11:32–33; Gal. 1:17), which were a natural extension of the environs of Judea, and would most likely lead to places such as the Hellenistic cities of eastern Syria, Armenia, Nisibis, Adiabene, Babylon, Susa, and perhaps even India.[3] There were, after all, a large Jewish diaspora (dispersion) and several Hellenistic cities in the east.[4]

During Paul's second missionary journey, when he and his companions are in the Phrygian part of Galatia, they attempt to go east into Bithynia, but Luke reports that 'the Spirit of Jesus did not let them' (Acts 16:7). Instead of going east, the Pauline mission goes west into Greece. Paul focuses his energies on establishing churches in the major cities of the Aegean coast, including Ephesus, Philippi, Thessalonica and Corinth. His use of main

---

3. R. Bauckham, 'What if Paul had Travelled East Rather Than West?', in *Virtual History and the Bible*, ed. J. C. Exum (Leiden: Brill, 1999), pp. 171–184.

4. See Josephus, *Ant.* 11.131–133; 18.34, 311–313, 379.

travel routes and major cities may represent a deliberate strategy to spread the Christian faith throughout the Roman Empire.[5] In the mid-50s AD, Paul writes to the Romans that 'from Jerusalem and as far around as Illyricum [modern Albania and the area near it] I have fully proclaimed the gospel of Christ' (Rom. 15:19). In fact, one of Paul's reasons for writing to the Romans is to garner their material support for his planned mission to Spain (Rom. 15:24–28). Spain is also known as 'Tarshish', and Isaiah 66:19 depicts Tarshish and Greece as the locations where the survivors of Israel's exile are sent in order to declare God's glory among the Gentiles. There is, then, some warrant for taking Isaiah 66:19 as providing the geographical framework for Paul's mission to take the gospel to the ends of the earth.[6]

Paul never presents a manifesto for mission, but the purpose of his apostolic call can be discerned in several of his passing remarks (1 Cor. 1:17; 9:19–23; 2 Cor. 5:11, 18–21; Rom. 1:5; 15:15–20; 16:26; Col. 1:28–29; Eph. 3:7–11; 6:19–20). In Romans, this is spelled out as bringing Gentiles into the 'obedience of faith' (Rom. 1:5; 16:26) and making them 'an offering acceptable to God' (Rom. 15:16). Salvation for Gentiles includes escape from God's wrath (1 Thess. 1:10; 5:9; Rom. 5:9), the forgiveness of sins, justification, redemption and reconciliation (Rom. 3 – 5; 2 Cor. 5:19–21; Gal. 2:15–21). The Gentiles also enter into the Abrahamic family (Rom. 4; Gal. 3 – 4) and join the commonwealth of Israel (Rom. 11:26; Gal. 6:16; Phil. 3:3; Eph. 2:11 – 3:6). This is achieved through the proclamation of Paul's gospel, which centres on the messianic identity and lordship of Jesus as well as the saving effects of his death and resurrection (Rom. 1:1–4; 1 Cor. 15:1–8; 2 Tim. 2:8). Paul is determined to preach the gospel where no apostle has gone before: he does not want to build on anyone else's foundation (Rom. 15:20–23; 2 Cor. 10:15–18). Divinely compelled to preach the gospel (1 Cor. 9:16; Eph. 6:19–20), Paul is motivated by a universal

5. W. M. Ramsay, *St. Paul the Traveller and Roman Citizen*, 11th ed. (London: Hodder & Stoughton, 1895).

6. R. Riesner, *Paul's Early Period: Chronology, Mission Strategy, Theology*, trans. D. Scott (Grand Rapids: Eerdmans, 1998), pp. 245–253.

concern to save as many people as possible (1 Cor. 9:19–23). He considers himself a vessel of God's power that will operate in him with great effect (Eph. 3:7; Col. 1:29).

According to Paul, the gospel is for the Jew first and then the Gentile (Rom. 1:16). This reflects both the geographical spread of the gospel from Judea to non-Jewish territory and also Paul's missionary strategy of using established Jewish communities as his starting point in a new city. Paul uses synagogues (Acts 9:20–25, 28–30; 13:5, 14–15; 14:1–7; 17:1, 10, 17; 18:4; 19:8; cf. Rom. 1:16; 1 Cor. 9:20; 2 Cor. 11:24) or his tent-making business (Acts 18:3; 20:33–35; cf. 1 Cor. 9:3–7; 2 Thess. 3:6–9) as avenues of contact with non-Jews. As such, Paul is an apostle not only *to* the Gentiles, but *among* them as well. However, the demarcation between Diaspora Jews (those living outside Palestine) and Gentiles was perhaps not as clear cut as in Palestine, especially when defining the *ethnē* ('nations' or 'Gentiles') politically or geographically.[7] Romans 1:5 can be translated, 'Through him and for the sake of his name, we received grace and apostleship to call people from among all the Gentiles (*en pasin tois ethnesin*) to the obedience that comes from faith.' Paul also refers in 1 Corinthians 9:20 to trying to win Jews and those under the law.

In Acts, the Diaspora Jews that Paul operates among are described as 'devout Jews from every nation' and the 'Jews living among the nations', showing that 'Jews' can be a subset of the foreign 'nations' (Acts 2:5; 21:21; cf. 9:15). But this must be balanced with the observation that in Acts the Diaspora Jews and their Gentile neighbours are usually distinguished from one another (Acts 13:46; 14:2, 5; 18:6; 26:23; cf. Gal. 2:7–16). Further proof that Paul's ministry is both to Jews of the Diaspora and to Gentiles is the fact that he experiences several heated clashes with Jewish-Christian missionaries who gravitate towards synagogue communities. Plus he earnestly pursues the unity of Jews and Gentiles in a common worship that is an issue only in a mixed Jewish–Gentile setting (see Galatians; 1 Cor. 8; and Rom. 14 – 15).

---

7. R. Strelan, *Paul, Artemis, and the Jews in Ephesus*, BZNW 80 (Berlin: W. de Gruyter, 1996), pp. 303–306.

Paul is not the first Christian missionary to go to the Gentiles (Acts 11:19–21) nor was he the only one (e.g. Acts 10 – 11; 15:39–41; Phil 1:15–18). Yet Paul retains a particular understanding of the significance of his own mission in the Mediterranean. He is not merely an apostle to the Gentiles but is *the* apostle to the Gentiles (Rom. 11:13; Gal. 2:8). And it is his mission to the Gentiles that will, he hopes, prompt national Israel finally to turn to the Messiah (Rom. 11:1–31). Plus Paul's sufferings absorb part of the messianic woes of the final tribulation (Col. 1:24). He is the custodian of the 'mystery' concerning the hardening of national Israel, the influx of Gentiles that will prompt Israel's final salvation (Rom. 11:25–26; 16:25) and the unity of Jews and Gentiles in one body (Eph. 3:3–6).

Paul's most profound theological statements derive from thinking on his feet while on the mission field. In the mission to the Gentiles, the apostle is forced to think through the deeper implications the gospel has for the lives of his Gentile converts, for his own ministry and how he relates to the concerns of Jews and Jewish Christians he encounters along the way. Martin Kähler is certainly right when he says mission is the 'mother of all theology'.[8] If that is true anywhere in the New Testament, it is certainly true of Paul.

Theologian

Paul is celebrated as the greatest theologian of the first-century church, and the depth of his intellect is perhaps matched only by Augustine in the fourth century. The study of Paul's theology is a battleground where skirmishes habitually take place over several key issues: the sources, shape, centre and development of his theology.

In terms of the *sources* of Paul's thought, several background areas have been proposed, including Hellenism, Cynicism, Stoicism, the Dead Sea Scrolls, Gnosticism, Rabbinic Judaism and

---

8. M. Kähler, *Schriften zur Christologie und Mission* (Munich: C. Kaiser, 1971 [1908]), p. 190.

Diaspora Judaism. But given that Paul has a foot in both the Jewish and Greek worlds, it is unsurprising that he echoes ideas contained in different intellectual forums. But to attribute his thinking to any one particular source runs into manifold problems. We must avoid the notion that analogy means genealogy or that similarity means source. Nor should we mistake the cultural context of Paul's thought with its content. More likely sources for Paul's theology include the following:

1. The Jesus tradition, or the body of Jesus' teaching transmitted in the early church, which informs significant parts of Paul's exhortations.
2. The Jewish Scriptures and Paul's reading of them through a Christocentric grid, which provides the substructure of his theology.
3. Paul's consistent application of the gospel to the situations he faces in order to ensure the vitality and integrity of the churches.

The *shape* of Paul's theology depends on whether we understand it as consisting of either apocalyptic themes and patterns that focus on the relationship between this age and the new age, or whether it consists principally of the redemptive-historical progress of salvation from Israel to the church through the coming of Christ. There is no need to make an either/or decision here, though, since Paul's apocalyptic eschatology and redemptive-historical motifs are linked in the narrative nature of Paul's theology. In Paul's letters, the implied stories of creation, Adam, Abraham and Israel find their definitive resolution in Christ. The story of Christ is really a story about the invasion of the future age into the present. This heavenly invasion brings with it a climax to these various substories, which results in the vindication of the covenant God and his new-covenant people.[9]

The *centre* of Paul's theology (*centrum Paulinium*) has had many

---

9. M. F. Bird, *The Saving Righteousness of God: Studies in Paul, Justification, and the New Perspective*, PBM (Milton Keynes: Paternoster, 2007), pp. 30–33.

proposals: justification by faith, participation in Christ, salvation-history, reconciliation and so on. Given the situational nature of Paul's letters and the fact that we have only windows into Paul and not Paul himself, it is most difficult to make any single theme the 'canon within the canon', so to speak. Can any single theme explain every single letter and every single passage? For instance, is justification by faith the centre of Philemon? While it perhaps sounds so general as to be meaningless, it may be better to say that 'Jesus Christ' is the centre of Paul's theology.[10] Christ is central in Paul's religious experience, proclamation and pastoral care. If we wanted to pursue something more specific, we could legitimately suggest that the death and resurrection of Jesus Christ are the main coordinates of his thinking, which would come close to iden-tifying the central theological thread in Paul's gospel.[11]

The question of the *development* of Paul's theology is a pertinent one. Scholars often argue that he changed his mind about the after-life from eschatological and linear categories in 1 Corinthians 15 to individual and spiritual categories in 2 Corinthians 5. Likewise, it is often supposed that Paul changes his mind about the law between Galatians and Romans. But Paul is a far more consistent thinker than many give him credit for, and the different emphases are prob-ably more attributable to the diverse circumstances he faces when penning each letter. Paul's theological framework is, I argue later, rooted in his Damascus road experience and never radically altered.[12] Still, we should not suppose that after regaining his sight in Damascus, he suddenly has the entire theological package worked out in detail, as if God magically downloaded the entire

---

10. J. Plevnik, 'The Center of Paul's Theology', *CBQ* 51 (1989), pp. 460–478; J. A. Fitzmyer, *Paul and His Theology: A Brief Sketch* (Englewood Cliffs: Prentice Hall, 1989); J. D. G. Dunn, *The Theology of Paul the Apostle* (Edinburgh: T. & T. Clark, 1998), p. 730.

11. C. E. B. Cranfield, *The Epistle to the Romans*, ICC, 2 vols. (Edinburgh: T. & T. Clark, 1975–9), vol. 2, pp. 826–835; J. C. Beker, *Paul the Apostle: The Triumph of God in the Life and Thought* (Philadelphia: Fortress, 1980), p. 207.

12. See recently S. Kim, *Paul and the New Perspective: Second Thoughts on the Origin of Paul's Gospel* (Grand Rapids: Eerdmans, 2002).

Westminster Confession or Thirty-Nine Articles into his brain.
There is no doubt in my mind that Paul's theology develops and
matures over time as he has to think and pray through the conflicts
and concerns posed by the various circumstances he faces, the
issues that emerge in the course of his ministry.

In sum, Paul is no ivory-tower theologian and his theological
reflection is done on the mission field and for the benefit of the
churches. He is essentially a theologian of the gospel, determined
to expound and apply the gospel to himself and his converts. Scot
McKnight aptly provides a basic rundown of Paul's theological
convictions:

> Paul's theology is not systematics; instead, he is grasped best when at least
> the following seven Pauline principles are kept on the table as we proceed
> through his letters. *First*, the gospel is the grace of God in revealing Jesus
> as Messiah and Lord for everyone who believes; *second*, everyone stands
> behind one of the twin heads of humanity, Adam and Christ; *third*, Jesus
> Christ is the centre stage, and it is participation in him that transfers a
> person from the Adam line to the Christ line; *fourth*, the church is the body
> of Christ on earth; *fifth*, (salvation-)history does not begin with Moses but
> with Abraham and the promise God gave to him, and finds its crucial
> turning point in Jesus Christ — but will run its course until the
> consummation in the glorious Lordship of Christ over all; *sixth*, Christian
> behaviour is determined by the Holy Spirit, not the Torah; *seventh*, Paul is
> an apostle and not a philosopher or systematic theologian. These principles
> spring into action when Paul meets his various threats (circumcision,
> wisdom, gifts, works of Torah, ethnocentrism, flesh, rival leaders, and
> eschatological fights about the Parousia or the general resurrection).[13]

Pastor

Although the letters 1–2 Timothy and Titus are usually called the
'Pastoral Epistles', this is somewhat a misnomer, since *all* of

---

13. S. McKnight, *Jesus and His Death: Historiography, the Historical Jesus, and
    Atonement Theory* (Waco: Baylor University Press, 2005), p. 374.

Paul's letters are pastoral in one sense or another. In the letters, we see Paul the pastor at work exhorting, encouraging and admonishing his converts and co-workers. The letters provide pastoral care when he is absent. As founder of several churches, Paul is their 'father' through the gospel (1 Cor. 4:15; Phil. 2:22). A snapshot of his ministry is given in Colossians: 'We proclaim him by instructing and teaching all persons with all wisdom in order that we might present every person perfect in Christ' (Col. 1:28).

This ministry is simultaneously evangelistic, didactic and pastoral. Paul is a church planter charged with establishing the foundations of a church in new regions (1 Cor. 3:6–11). Both he and his delegates visit the churches and teach them at length in order to 'establish you in your faith and to exhort you' (1 Thess. 3:2). One of the most poignant images of Paul in his letters is that of a parent desperately concerned about his children (2 Cor. 6:13; 12:14; 1 Thess. 2:11; Phlm. 10). Elsewhere we encounter maternal language in Paul's affection and angst for his converts (1 Cor. 3:1–3; Gal. 4:19; 1 Thess. 2:7). Among his many travails and sufferings, Paul lists his frantic concern for the churches: 'And, besides other things, I am under daily pressure because of my anxiety for all the churches. Who is weak, and I am not weak? Who is made to stumble, and I am not inflamed?' (2 Cor. 11:28–29). In the context of 2 Corinthians 11, we could argue it is pastoral care of this kind (and not simply signs and wonders) that are the surest indicator of his being an authentic apostle.[14]

It is equally vital to understand Paul's pastoral concern in the light of his eschatological framework. He will boast of his converts on the Day of Christ Jesus (2 Cor. 1:14; Phil. 2:16), and on the Day of Judgment Paul's converts will be his joy and crown (1 Thess. 2:19–20; Phil. 4:1). The lives they have lived will indicate whether or not Paul has laboured in vain (Phil. 2:16), and the foundations he has used to build up converts will be tested by fire (1 Cor. 3:10–15). Paul claims he betrothed his converts to

---

14. P. Beasley-Murray, 'Pastor, Paul as', in *DPL*, ed. G. F. Hawthorne, R. P. Martin and D. G. Reid (Downers Grove and Leicester: IVP, 1993), p. 655.

Christ and that he alone will present them to him at the final recompense (2 Cor. 11:1–3). The future will bring to light the success of his pastorate and the succour he has provided his converts.

Paul's pastoral concern is an outworking of his gospel ministry. He rebukes Peter for not 'walking towards the truth of the gospel' when the integrity of the Gentile Christians in Antioch is endangered by those of the circumcision group who want Gentiles to become proselytes to Judaism (Gal. 2:14). In Acts, Luke narrates Paul's impassioned address, anchored in Paul's testimony to the 'gospel of grace' (Acts 20:24), to the elders of the church of Ephesus about protecting the flock from wolves. Paul aspires for his converts to live a life 'worthy of the gospel' (Phil. 1:27), exercising obedience that accompanies 'confession of the gospel' (2 Cor. 9:13). I have argued elsewhere that Paul writes to the Romans, to a cluster of churches he did not establish, as part of an exercise in preventative pastoral care.[15]

Paul has intended to visit Rome in person to impart some spiritual gift to the saints there, but in lieu of that decides to encourage and put them in his debt by explicating his gospel to them in the hope of transforming their potentially fractious cosmopolitan community into one where Christian Jews and Gentiles are united in common worship by a common gospel (Rom. 1:11–12). Paul aspires to 'gospelize' the Romans so that the truth and ramifications of the gospel will work themselves out in relations among members of the community.[16] About pastoral ministry, and the gospel more generally, Derek Tidball writes, 'The gospel determines everything about the pastor – his motives, authority, methods, and character are all governed by the good news of Jesus Christ.'[17] If that is true of any pastor it is true of Paul. Fitting also are the words of Ernest Best:

---

15. Bird, *Saving Righteousness of God*, pp. 140–141.
16. I owe the term 'gospelize' to my former theology professor, Revd Jim Gibson of Malyon College in Brisbane, Australia. For more about this term, see chapter 10 below.
17. D. Tidball, *Skilful Shepherds: Explorations in Pastoral Theology* (Leicester: Apollos, 1997), p. 120.

'We often thank God for Paul the theologian and Paul the missionary pioneer. I believe we can also thank God for Paul the pastor,
who so demonstrated his care that his churches grew, and left an
example so that the church continues to mature.'[18]

Martyr

Paul's experience of persecution, hardship and suffering influence
his view of his ministry and his expectations of his converts. He
refers to the sufferings of Christ overflowing into both his own life
and that of his co-workers (2 Cor. 1:5–11). He catalogues the
various sufferings he has faced (1 Cor. 4:11–13; 2 Cor. 11:23–30)
and regards his sufferings as even absorbing the messianic woes of
the tribulation (Col. 1:24). Paul likens his ministry to a triumphal
procession, where the captives are led in chains to their execution
behind the chariot of a conquering king returning to his home city
(1 Cor. 4:9). During one period of captivity, the apostle is aware he
may die (Phil. 1:20–26). Despite this, Paul's imprisonment serves
to advance the gospel and spur others on to speak the word more
boldly (Phil. 1:12–14).

In the Thessalonian correspondence, trials are something
Christians are destined for (1 Thess. 3:3) and require perseverance
(2 Thess. 1:4). The same persecutions and sufferings Paul and the
churches of Judea experience are shared by the churches Paul has
founded (1 Thess. 1:6; 2:14; Phil. 1:29–30). Some believers have
been counted as worthy to suffer for Christ (2 Thess. 1:5; Phil.
1:30). Paul commends the Macedonian churches for their generosity despite poverty and persecution (2 Cor. 8:1–5). The suffering
theme becomes more acute in the Pastoral Epistles, where
suffering is a result of testifying to the gospel (2 Tim. 1:8, 12; 2:9).
For Paul, then, suffering is part of the Christian life in general and
the apostolic office in particular.[19]

-----

18. E. Best, *Paul and his Converts* (Edinburgh: T. & T. Clark, 1988), p. 161.
19. See recently, L. A. Jervis, *At the Heart of the Gospel: Suffering in the Earliest
    Christian Message* (Grand Rapids: Eerdmans, 2007).

We have no biblical account of what happens to Paul beyond
the two years he spends under house arrest in Rome around AD
60–2 (Acts 28:14–31). However, the Pastoral Epistles seem to
imply a release from prison, a subsequent ministry in Miletus
(2 Tim. 4:20), Troas (2 Tim. 4:13), Macedonia (1 Tim. 1:3) and
Crete (Tit. 1:5), followed up with a second Roman imprisonment,
when the Pastorals are written. Clement, writing in Rome at the
end of the first century, writes this of Paul's death:

> Paul by his example pointed out the way to the prize for patient
> endurance. After he had been seven times in chains, had been driven into
> exile, had been stoned, and had preached in the East and in the West, he
> won the genuine glory for his faith, having taught righteousness to the
> whole world and having reached the farthest limits of the West. Finally,
> when he had given his testimony before the rulers, he thus departed
> from the world and went to the holy place, having become an
> outstanding example of patient endurance.
>
> (*1 Clem.* 5:5–7)

This reference to the 'extreme limit of the west' may suggest that
Paul did make it as far as Spain, although this is more likely a
reference to Rome. The Muratorian Fragment, a second-century
preface to a collection of the New Testament writings, makes
explicit reference to Paul's journey to Spain. But it is difficult to
accommodate a trip to Spain and subsequent missionary efforts
there in addition to Paul's travels to Asia Minor between a first and
second Roman imprisonment. More likely, a trip to Spain was an
inference that Christian authors made based on their reading of
Romans 15:24, 28. The tradition that Paul was beheaded in Rome
during the bloodthirsty persecutions of Nero in the mid- to late
60s AD is certainly plausible (Eusebius, *Hist. eccl.* 2.25.5–8). A leg-
endary account of Paul's martyrdom is contained in a second- or
third-century work called *The Martyrdom of Paul*.[20] Paul is sum-
moned before Nero in chains, the apostle gives an impassioned

---

20. Usually co-located with the *Acts of Paul and Thecla* and *3 Corinthians* in a
    composite work called *The Acts of Paul*.

speech about serving Christ and is beheaded. After his beheading, milk gushes out from his neck. The story is an elaborate fiction but one that greatly influenced later Christian art.

During my childhood years my aunt and uncle had three friendly Labradors, one of whom was named 'Nero'. I had always thought that Nero was an odd name for a dog, especially when names like 'Rover' or 'Fido' were more common. There is, however, a comic irony behind naming a dog Nero. I happened upon this irony when I read a quote by T. R. Glover, who noted the fact that Paul the apostle was put to death under the reign of Nero in the 60s AD, yet the day was to come when men would call their sons 'Paul' and their dogs 'Nero'.[21]

Conclusion

Up to this point we have looked at the conundrums of studying Paul, asked why we should study him, and looked at several images of him in the New Testament: persecutor, missionary, theologian, pastor and martyr. We might now add another image: *maverick*. Paul was regarded by many Jewish Christians as a meddlesome nonconformist, by Jews as a blasphemous apostate, and by Roman authorities as a mischievous nuisance. There is no doubt that Paul was a controversialist and we may even speak of his abrasive personality (cf. Gal. 2:11–14; Acts 15:35–41). The chief legacy of Paul is his claim that Gentiles can be part of the Israel of God without becoming proselytes to Judaism. He also claims that there is another 'Lord', one who rivals Caesar and who will establish an everlasting kingdom that will overthrow all despots and self-divinized pretenders (Phil. 2:10–11; Acts 17:7).

Paul is not given the thirty-nine lashes by his fellow Jews because he asks them to 'try' Jesus in the same way one might try a kebab (2 Cor. 11:24). He is not executed for suggesting that Roman citizens may wish to invite Jesus into their hearts. No, Paul

21. Cited from F. F. Bruce, *Paul: Apostle of the Free Spirit*, rev. ed. (Carlisle, UK: Paternoster, 1980), p. 5.

has the courage and conviction to proclaim that the one who is to come again, the Messiah, is Jesus, who has fulfilled Israel's hopes by being cursed on a cross and raised from the dead. Jesus is the deliverer Israel has hoped for and desperately needed (2 Cor. 1:20; Acts 13:32–34; Rom. 11:26).

Paul dares to defy an empire by claiming that the seat of judgment is occupied by Jesus Christ and not by Caesar (Rom. 14:10; 2 Cor. 5:10). The answer to the perils of human existence is not subjugation to and worship of Rome, but faith in Jesus the Christ. Paul never gets over the fact that he has been saved by the same God he once strenuously opposed in his persecution of Christians. For Paul, grace is an event he experienced on the road to Damascus (Gal. 1:15), and it compels him to try to save as many as possible (1 Cor. 9.22). God's grace is the reason Paul considers his death as 'gain' (Phil. 1:21), and why he construes his identity as being bound up with the cross of Christ (Gal. 2:19–20). Paul is, in his own words, 'a servant of Jesus Christ'. His journey is well worth exploring in greater depth.

2. A FUNNY THING HAPPENED ON THE ROAD TO DAMASCUS

Paul's life was dramatic, to say the least. The most dramatic event was, of course, his Christophany, or encounter with the risen Christ, on the road to Damascus. But this event must be situated in the wider context of Paul's career. The problem is that trying to reconstruct Paul's chronology from his epistles and from Acts is like trying to piece together two jumbled jigsaws, while at the same time knowing that pieces from both jigsaws are missing. For instance, does the meeting in Galatians 2:1–10 correspond to the Jerusalem council of Acts 15 or does it correspond to the famine relief visit of Acts 11:28–30? Fortunately, there are three anchor points we can firmly tie Paul to:

1. The Nabataean King Aretas died between AD 38 and 40, and Nabataean control of Damascus is unlikely before AD 37, when Caligula acceded to the throne in Rome (2 Cor. 11:32–33 = Acts 9:24–25).
2. The expulsion of the Jews from Rome under Caligula occurred in AD 49 (Suetonius, *Claud.* 25.4), which is treated as recent in Acts 18:2 when Paul encounters Priscilla and Aquila in Corinth.

3. The proconsulship of Gallio in Achaia can be dated to AD 51–52
    due to inscriptional evidence that sets Paul's ministry in Corinth
    within that period (Acts 18:11–13).

An overview of Paul's chronology looks something like this:

Biography

Birth of Paul	5 BC to AD 10
Death of Jesus	AD 29/30
Persecution of Christians	30–33
Conversion	33
Ministry in Arabia/Damascus	34–37
Jerusalem (1st visit)	37
Syria and Cilicia	37–46
Antioch	47
Jerusalem (2nd visit)	48
First missionary journey	48
Antioch (confronts Peter, Gal. 2:11–14)	48

Epistle to the Galatians

Apostolic Council (Acts 15)	49–50
Second missionary journey	50–52
Travels through Macedonia/Greece	51–52

1–2 Thessalonians

Antioch via Jerusalem (Acts 18:22)	52
Third missionary journey	53–57
Time at Ephesus	53–55

1–2 Corinthians

Philippi	55
Corinth	55–56

Epistle to the Romans

Jerusalem (final trip)	57
Imprisonment in Caesarea Maritima	57–59
Journey to Rome	59–60
House arrest in Rome	60–62

Colossians, Philippians, Philemon
Further missionary travels in Asia Minor   62–64
Nero's pogrom against Christians   64–65
Second imprisonment in Rome   65–68

Ephesians, Pastoral Epistles
Execution by beheading   67–68

Persecutor to preacher

Sometime around AD 33 Saul of Tarsus experienced an encounter with the risen Lord Jesus. It turned his world upside down and transformed the zealous *persecutor* of the church into one of its most ardent *proclaimers*. In order to understand the mammoth reversal in Paul's life and allegiances, we have to contrast who Paul was prior to the Damascus road experience with who he became afterwards. We have already noted several of Paul's remarks about his pre-Christian life (e.g. Gal. 1:13–14; Phil. 3:5–7; 1 Cor. 15:9) and can make several observations based on this.

First, the pre-Christian Paul was a pious Jew who endeavoured to live his life according to the will of God set out in the Law and Prophets. He followed the Pharisaic model for living that life as directed by the traditions of the elders. Paul was not a Jew waiting for a divine Messiah to cleanse his burdened conscience of sin; on the contrary, he considered himself 'blameless' (Phil. 3:6).

Second, we should ask why Paul persecuted the church? It is not because the first Christians had completely forsaken the Jewish law. Acts 1 – 5 represents the early church as resolutely devout in its law observance and worship in the temple. Even the idea of believing in a messiah would not prompt immediate action, as quasi-messianic pretenders popped up occasionally. Several factors, however, did contribute to his militant action.

1. Belief in a *crucified* Messiah was scandalous (cf. 1 Cor. 1:18–23; Rom. 9:32–33; Gal. 5:11; 6:12–14; Phil. 3:18). But why? In short, the Messiah was meant to be the representative of Israel par excellence, thus '[t]he cross is offensive to Jews because a crucified

Messiah implies a crucified Israel'.[1] A crucified Messiah forces a dramatic redrawing of core Jewish beliefs about kingship, vindication, eschatology, restoration and the fate of the Gentiles.

2. Another reason for persecution is that, soon after his death, some followers of Jesus began incorporating Jesus into patterns of religious devotion normally reserved for Yahweh. This is evident from the formula 'in the name of Jesus' used in baptisms, prayers, healings and exorcisms (e.g. Acts 2:38; 4:30; 10:48; 16:18; 19:5, 17) and invocation made to Jesus in Aramaic-speaking worship as *maranatha*, 'our Lord come' (e.g. 1 Cor. 16:22; Rev. 22:20; *Did.* 10.6) (see more on this in chapter 8 below).

3. Saul was zealous for Torah, which meant something more than possessing buckets of enthusiasm for Moses. To be zealous meant a willingness to use violence against other Jews who threatened the sanctity of Israel's separation from Gentiles. For example, during Israel's wilderness wanderings, the priest Phinehas manifested 'zeal' by killing an Israelite man who was having intercourse with a foreign woman (Num. 25:11). During the forced Hellenization of Judea by the Seleucid King Antiochus Epiphanes IV (167–64 BC), an old priest named Mattathias exhibited a similar violent zeal against a fellow Jew who attempted to offer a pagan sacrifice (1 Macc. 2.24–26, 50, 58). Thus, Paul's 'zeal' was aimed against Christians who, in his mind, threatened the integrity of the boundaries that separated Jews from Gentiles and endangered the holiness of the Jewish people.

The catalyst for Saul's persecution was probably the Greek-speaking Jewish Christians who had begun proclaiming Jesus to Gentiles, welcoming them into the people of God without making them enter via the route of conversion to Judaism (Acts 11:19–21). To suggest that 'sinners' or 'Gentiles' could stand before God on the same footing as Jews but without actually becoming Jews was to lower the currency of Israel's election. It devalued the covenant marker of circumcision and would lead to Jews fraternizing too much with Gentiles. However, the saving

---

1. N. T. Wright, 'The Paul of History and the Apostle of Faith', *TynBul* 29 (1978), p. 68.

righteousness of God accomplishes just such a social transformation: it acquits both Jews and Gentiles from the verdict of God's judgment and allows them both to be adopted into the multi-ethnic family of God. Martin Hengel writes:

> For the most part Pauline theology rests on the radical reversal of former values and aims which came about through the encounter with the crucified and risen Jesus of Nazareth. The Jewish teacher becomes the missionary to the Gentiles; the 'zeal for the law' is replaced by the proclamation of the gospel without the law; justification of the righteous on the basis of their 'works of the law' is replaced by justification of the 'godless' through faith alone; the free will is replaced by the faith which is given by grace alone as the creation of the word; and hatred of the crucified and accursed pseudo-messiah is replaced by a theology of the cross which grounds the salvation of all men and women in the representative accursed death of the messiah on the cross.[2]

Paul never recounts the exact circumstances of his encounter with Christ, but does offer a few snippets along the way as to what happened. In Galatians, we are told, 'But when God, who had set me apart before I was born and called me through his grace, was pleased to reveal his Son *in me*' (Gal. 1:15–16). In 1 Corinthians 9:1, he states that he has 'seen Jesus our Lord'. Then in 1 Corinthians 15:8–9, Paul lists the witnesses to the resurrection and includes himself: 'Last of all, as to one untimely born, he appeared also to me. For I am the least of the apostles, unfit to be called an apostle, because I persecuted the church of God.' That phrase 'one untimely born' is the same word used for an abortion or miscarriage (*ektrōma*).[3] This violent image Paul uses to describe his own experience pertains to an endangered infant being ripped out of the womb and brought into the light.

Was Paul converted to a new religion or was he called to

---

2. M. Hengel, *The Pre-Christian Paul*, trans. J. Bowden (London: SCM, 1991), p. 86.

3. For the evidence from Acts about Paul's conversion see Acts 9:1–21; 22:1–21; 26:2–23.

missionary service? While it has been fashionable in recent decades to say that Paul was 'called' rather than 'converted', we might remember that Paul's gut-wrenching and decisive transformation meant he was indeed swung around 180 degrees.[4] This conversion, however, was not a conversion from one religion to another or from Judaism to Christianity. Paul was converted from the Pharisaic sect to a messianic sect *within Judaism*. At this juncture, Paul became what sociologists call a 'deviant' or 'defector' in the eyes of his Pharisaic contemporaries. And with that dramatic reorientation came a call to a specific mission, namely to be Christ's apostle to the Gentiles. Both Paul and Luke declare that Paul's commission to go to the Gentiles is given during his Christophany (Gal. 1:16; Acts 26:17–18).[5] This call is formulated in language reminiscent of the call of Old Testament prophets (e.g. Isa. 42:1–7; 49:1–7; Jer. 1:4–5), since it parallels the arresting nature of the prophetic call and the charge to be an agent of salvation and covenant renewal (Acts 13:47/Isa. 49:6; Rom. 15:21/Isa. 52:15).

What changes took place in Paul's theological beliefs at this point? While we must leave room for learning, development, reflection and maturation, we cannot underestimate the instantaneous theological shockwaves that reverberated through his mind in that encounter, the effects of which remained with him for the rest of his life.

1. In terms of *Christology* (beliefs about the person of Christ), Paul had to come to grips with the fact that Jesus was not a false prophet or a messianic pretender but, on the contrary, was the risen and exalted Son of God (Rom. 1:4; Gal. 2:20; 2 Cor. 1:19).

---

4. A. F. Segal, *Paul the Convert: The Apostolate and Apostasy of Saul the Pharisee* (New Haven: Yale University Press, 1990), pp. 5–7.

5. Alternatively, see Acts 22:15, 21, which could imply that the Gentile mission was based on a subsequent revelation Paul received in Jerusalem, and that it became apparent to him only later on that it was an aspect of his calling. I am more disposed to think that the revelation to go to the Gentiles was part of the Damascus road experience, since Paul's first period of ministry was in Damascus and Arabia/Nabataea (Gal. 1:17; 2 Cor. 11:32; Acts 9:19–25), a region largely comprising non-Jews.

The experience would remain indelibly imprinted in Paul's mind and meant that Christ was to be identified with God's own glory (2 Cor. 4:4–6; 8:23; Rom. 16:27; Phil. 4:19; 2 Thess. 2:14; Eph. 1:12; Tit. 2:13).

2. On his *soteriology* (beliefs about salvation), Paul previously believed in covenantal grace alongside Torah-obedience as the determining factors for salvation. After the Damascus road experience, he believed salvation to be from Christ and nowhere else. Paul knew that Jesus was hanged on a cross and also knew that Deuteronomy 21:23 said that anyone hanged on a tree is under God's curse. But if Jesus was cursed, he must have been cursed by God the Father, and God must have cursed him for a specific reason. The reason was that 'Christ redeemed us from the curse of the law by becoming a curse for us' (Gal. 3:13).

3. Regarding *eschatology* (beliefs about the future age), Paul formerly believed as a Pharisee that God would resurrect all humans at the end of history and vindicate those who had remained faithful to the covenant. Instead, God had raised up one man in the middle of history and vindicated him. Which is why Christ is the one through whom 'the end of ages has come' (1 Cor. 10:11), as his resurrection and the bequeathing of the Spirit mark the partial arrival of the future age in the here and now. This is confirmed by his remarks that Christ is the first fruits (1 Cor. 15:20, 23) or firstborn (Rom. 8:29; Col. 1:15, 18) of the new creation, and the Spirit is the deposit of the new age yet to come in its fullness (2 Cor. 1:22; 5:5; Eph. 1:13–14).

4. There were seismic shifts on Paul's *nomology* (beliefs about the law). Previously, Paul believed that law or Torah marked out the people of God and obedience to its precepts was the basis upon which God would justify or vindicate his people. Now this is replaced by faith in the Messiah. It is faith alone that determines membership in the people of God and is the basis for God's verdict of acquittal. Which is why he can argue against his fellow Jews that Christ is the 'end of the law', or the goal to which it was headed (Rom. 10:4). Against his fellow Jewish Christians he can also argue that Jesus is not an add-on to Moses, for Jesus inaugurates a whole new epoch of 'faith' (Gal. 3:23–24). Whereas many Jews believed that God's wisdom was incarnated in the law of Moses (Sir. 24.1–23;

Bar. 3.29 – 4.1; 4 Macc. 1.16–17), Paul came to believe that Christ is the embodiment of God's wisdom (1 Cor. 1:30). As the Jewish scholar Claude Montefiore put it, 'Christianity is not the Law plus Christ. It is Jesus Christ alone.'[6]

5. On the subject of *ecclesiology* (beliefs about the church), Paul had persecuted Christians and yet the risen Jesus asked him, 'Why do you persecute me?' The implication being that by persecuting Christians, Paul was persecuting Jesus. That immediately implied that Christians were in some sense the 'body of Christ' (e.g. Rom. 12:5; 1 Cor. 10:16; 12:12–13, 27; Eph. 5:23). What is more, if Messiah rather than Torah is the defining element for salvation, then it means salvation is opened up for the Gentiles without coming under the wings of Torah.

The pre-Christian Paul was not like a Josephus or a Justin Martyr, who were busy trying all assorted religious sects and philosophies until one finally took their fancy. Paul was not a spiritual seeker who happened upon Jesus; he was a zealous Pharisee convinced that by crushing this pernicious sect he was doing his countrymen and God a favour. In fact, he was probably the last person anyone would have expected to become a follower of Jesus and dedicate the rest of his life to testifying among Jews and Gentiles that Jesus is the Messiah (as Acts 9:26–27 and Gal. 1:23–24 make clear).

But what caused Paul to reconfigure his biography, reverse his allegiances and pursue the proclamation of the good news in the face of deadly opposition? The answer is that a ferocious force had seized and turned him inside out, upside down, and spun him round half a dozen times. This encounter with the risen Jesus had an enormous impact on his continuing religious experience of God, on his missionary drive and upon his theological reflection about God, Israel, Torah and salvation. That grace-event killed Saul the Pharisee and birthed Paul the apostle.

---

6. C. G. Montefiore, *Judaism and St. Paul: Two Essays* (London: Macmillan, 1914), p. 129.

3. THE STORIES BEHIND THE STORY

In the letters of Paul we encounter a number of stories lurking beneath the text. First, there is the story of Paul himself and the events of his life and ministry. Second, we have the various stories of Paul's converts and his relationship with them. But behind all of this is a deeper and more penetrating story with a number of subplots and sequels, a grand narrative we might call 'redemptive history'. In short, redemptive history is the story of creation and new creation or of the journey from Eden to New Jerusalem. The main chapters of that story are 'God and creation', 'Adam and Christ', 'Abraham', 'Israel', 'Jesus' and 'The church'.

These miniature narratives are embedded in Paul's letters and Paul consciously echoes, evokes and retells them as part of his theological and pastoral task. His epistles are not a pool of timeless theological and moral truths; instead, they are a form of personal communication between Paul and his readers. And yet they bring to light an underlying story, a story of God and the ways in which his purposes are unfolding. Understanding these narratives will help us to grasp Paul's theology far better. Beliefs and doctrines are not forged amid a list of propositions and by logical inferences, but in the telling of a story.

Story is the most characteristic expression of world view and identity. It defines who we are, where we come from, what the problem is and where we are going. Rituals are often employed to assist communities in telling their story. The Passover, for example, reminded the Israelites of the exodus from Egypt, while the Lord's Supper reminds Christians of Calvary. Both meals tell the story of God's deliverance of his people from bondage and slavery. One has only to read the words of Deuteronomy 26:5–9 or 1 Corinthians 11:23–26 to see how a particular story charged an ordinary meal with extraordinary significance. The invitation to believe in Jesus and join the church was ultimately an invitation to identify with a certain story and to order one's life according to the story, symbols and praxis of Jesus the Messiah. As the old hymn goes, 'We have a story to tell the nations', a story that reaches back to Genesis and culminates in Christ handing the kingdom back to the Father: that is the story world of Paul, the story we must grapple with if we are to understand him properly.

God and creation

In the Old Testament, God is the Creator of 'heaven and earth' (e.g. Gen. 14:19, 22; 24:3; Ps. 115:15) and thus is separate from creation, superior to creation and sovereign over creation. Genesis 1 indicates that creation was a good thing, reflecting the very goodness of God himself. Sin was an alien intrusion into God's world, and death was an equally unwelcome consequence. That God is Creator is axiomatic for Paul, and rejection of God as Creator is the root of all human wickedness (Rom. 1:20–25). While not discounting the importance of Christ, we cannot set aside the theocentric nature of Paul's theology. In Romans, the word 'God' (*theos*) occurs 153 times. Note the steady stream of genitival phrases: gospel *of* God, son *of* God, beloved *of* God, will *of* God, power *of* God, righteousness *of* God, wrath *of* God, glory *of* God, truth *of* God, judgment *of* God – Romans is fundamentally God-talk!

Furthermore, in Romans this God-talk is steeped in Jewish

tradition: God who is blessed forever (1:25; 9:5), God will judge the world (3:5), God who gives life to the dead (4:17), God who searches the heart (8:27), the doxology to God (11:33–36), God of peace (16:20) and eternal God (16:26). Paul is a devout monotheist too: God is one (3:30), he is 'the only wise God' (16:27) and as a result there can be no other gods (1:22–23). We also observe from Romans that humanity has become alienated from God due to sin and has earned the wrath of God (1:18–32), while creation itself is longing for redemption and restoration (8:19–23). The story goes: God is Creator; all creatures and even creation itself are tainted by sin, marred by corruption and alienated from God; but God intends to restore creation to its period of Edenic goodness and glory through the revelation of his righteousness in the death and resurrection of Christ.

Adam and Christ

John Milton wrote in *Paradise Lost*:

> Of man's first disobedience, and the fruit
> Of that forbidden tree, whose mortal taste
> Brought death into the world and all our woe,
> With loss of Eden, till one greater Man
> Restore us, and regain the blissful seat.
> (1:1–6)

Milton captures perfectly the sombre mood of the story of Genesis 3. Adam's fall and its effect upon the human race is presupposed and portrayed at several junctures in Paul's letters, including 1 Corinthians 11 and 15, Romans 5 and 1 Timothy 2. In the midst of arguing for the resurrection of the dead in 1 Corinthians 15, Paul writes, 'For as through a man death came, by a man has the resurrection of the dead also come. For just as in Adam all die, so also in Christ all will be made alive' (1 Cor. 15:21–22).

The basic thread of this story is that of our bond and solidarity with Adam, resulting in our death. Not only is that bond broken, but it is also overturned and reversed by the new bond established with Christ, who makes us alive in the face of death. The contrast is continued in verses 45–49, where humans are freed from the decay and death of the 'man of dust' and share in the immortal life of the 'man from heaven'. We find the same theme in Romans 5:12–21, where the first Adam is a type, pattern or prototype of the New Adam, who is Christ. Romans 5:12–21 has a lot to say about the entrance and effect of Adam's sin and how Christ overturns the consequences of that sin. In verse 12 we can detect a particular line of thought:

1. Sin entered the world through Adam.
2. Death is the consequence of the sin of Adam.
3. Death has spread to the whole human race.
4. Human beings, because they enter the world alienated from God, sin.

What is the relationship between Adam's sin and the sins of humanity? Do we receive merely a sinful nature from Adam or do we receive both a sinful nature and his verdict of condemnation already upon us at birth? This is one of many battlegrounds between theologians about the origin of sin, and much of it depends on how one understands the transmission of sin and how one translates a rather enigmatic phrase '*because* all sinned' (*eph ho pantes hēmarton*) in Romans 5:12. Yet we might keep in mind that this debate was not unique to Christianity, as many Jews themselves differed on the relationship between Adam's transgression and the force it exerted on human sin.

> O Adam, what have you done? For though it was you who sinned, the fall was not yours alone, but ours also who are your descendants.
>   (*4 Ezra* 7.118)

> For, although Adam sinned first and has brought death upon all who were not in his own time, yet each of them has been born from him and has prepared for himself the coming torment.
>   (*2 Bar.* 54.15)

The document *4 Ezra* assumes that Adam's sin belongs to everyone or becomes their possession in some form. In contrast,

2 Baruch contends that while Adam's sin brought death into the world, the punishment for sin is ultimately one's own responsibility, so we bear the punishment for our own sins, not necessarily Adam's sin. So which is it? The problem is that Paul does not say explicitly what the connection is between Adam's sin and the sins of humanity, but a link is definitely presupposed.

What we have here is probably a conception of corporate personality and federal representation, as Adam was the human representative, and what is true of him, alienation and condemnation, becomes true of others as well because they are born in Adam. The sins human beings commit against God and against each other are a re-enactment and ratification of Adam's sin in their own person, proving they truly are sons of Adam and daughters of Eve.

The argument of Romans 5:12–21 involves a *synkrisis*, or comparison between the two 'types' or figures, Adam and Christ. In Adam, we have a story of a world gone horribly wrong. As the one who was made to rule over creation is now subject to it, he forfeits his wonderful privileges of intimate fellowship with God. He suffers a severe loss of fortunes, loses divine favour, is exiled from paradise, and even his own being becomes disfigured and corrupted. The one created for immortality experiences the painful horror of death, and so do all of his offspring, as they share his guilt and new-found disposition towards evil. It is not blessings but sins that are multiplied to future generations, as humanity forgets and then forsakes God altogether and so recapitulates the story of Adam's disobedience in their own persons. Death begets death. Sin dehumanized humanity, so that, despite possessing the divine image, they act like little more than complex beasts, fighting and devouring one another.

But in Christ we have a story of a world put right, as Christ is faithful where Adam was faithless, and is obedient where Adam was disobedient. Through his act of righteous obedience, Jesus overturns the transgression of Adam and so is able to deliver and transform the fallen progeny of Adam. Christ creates in himself a new humanity, which, through the renewing power of the Spirit, is able to undo the effects of the fall and become the new Adamic race.

In want of a modern analogy, George Lucas's six-part saga *Star Wars* can be called a 'Tale of Two Skywalkers', and in many ways mirrors the Adam–Christ contrast of Romans 5 and 1 Corinthians 15, where Adam and Christ stand for the two respective heads of humanity. They are representatives or *types* of either a corrupted humanity (Adam) or a redeemed humanity (Christ). The first Skywalker (Anakin Skywalker) faced the temptation to give in to the dark side of the force: he gave in to it and death, destruction and chaos followed. In contrast, the second Skywalker (Luke Skywalker) faced the same temptation, but was faithful and obedient to the Jedi vocation, and consequently hope, life and the triumph of good followed. In fact, Luke was able to redeem the first Skywalker, his father Anakin, from evil through his faithfulness.

Christ, the second Adam, delivers the offspring of Adam from their sin by his faithfulness and obedience. Thus, the story goes, Adam sinned and because Adam is humanity's representative his sin is counted as theirs. Humanity receives from Adam a verdict of condemnation upon it and an inherited propensity to sin. Whereas the disobedience of the first Adam brought sin, condemnation and death, the faithfulness of the second Adam brings righteousness, vindication and eternal life (see chapter 6 below).

Abraham

'Father Abraham had many sons, many sons had father Abraham': so the song goes. But who are the children of Abraham? That was a question Jews debated among themselves, and it was ultimately a question that separated Jews and Christians from one another. A big subject the first Christians had to wrestle with was how the new covenant instituted by Jesus relates to the law of Moses and the promises made to Abraham. Do you need Jesus and Moses in order to be a son of Abraham? The story of Abraham is of tremendous significance for Paul and his churches, as the story of Abraham determines who they are and what is required of them to become the people of God.

In Genesis, Abraham is called by God to leave his father and homeland with the promise that he will be made into a great nation and all peoples of the earth will be blessed through him (Gen. 12:1–3). God establishes a covenant with Abraham that also includes the promise of land (Gen. 15:7–21; 17:2, 4, 8), and later circumcision is given as the sign of the covenant (Gen. 17:9–21). Abraham is tested by God concerning his willingness to offer up his son Isaac as a sacrifice (called the Aqedah, 'binding') and is found faithful, God himself providing the sacrifice (Gen. 22:1–18).

The significance of Abraham in the Hebrew Scriptures is that he was the father of the Jewish people, the source of their promises of land and descendants and the one through whom God would bless the nations. Jewish interpretation of Abraham during the Second Temple period was commonplace, as Abraham was a celebrated figure of Israel's heritage and his story was often retold to encourage Jews to be faithful and righteous. In many ways, these retellings of the Abraham story stand in direct contrast to how Paul used the Abraham story in his epistles. For instance, whereas Joshua 24:2–3 depicts Abraham as called out of idolatry, some Jewish authors regarded Abraham as being against idolatry prior to his call, so that God rewarded him with blessings and a covenant.

First, a document called *Jubilees* says that as a young boy Abraham recognized that 'everyone [has gone] astray after graven images and after pollution' (*Jub.* 11.16). As a grown man Abraham begged his father, Terah, a pagan priest, to cease idolatry and worship God (*Jub.* 12.1–8). In Pseudo-Philo, Abraham is among a few of Noah's descendants who refuse to participate in the construction of the tower of Babel (*LAB* 6.3–18). In the *Apocalypse of Abraham*, Abraham mocks the idols of his father (*Apoc. Ab.* 4.3 – 6:19).

Second, references to Abraham's obedience and righteousness were reiterated in the Hebrew Scriptures (Gen. 26:4–5; Neh. 9:7–8), but some Jewish authors went so far as to argue that Abraham kept the law of Moses. In Sirach it states, 'He kept the law of the Most High, and entered into a covenant with him' (Sir. 44.20). The logic being, (1) Abraham pleased God, (2) you please God by keeping the law, and (3) therefore, Abraham kept the law. The fact that the law was introduced 430 years later did not seem to bother them; after all, why let chronology interfere with good theology? It is tacitly supposed that Abraham must have had a private revelation of the law and been obedient to it. How else can someone please God?

Genesis 15:6 (a key verse for Paul in Rom. 4 and Gal. 3) records that 'Abram believed the LORD, and he credited it to him as right-eousness.' In Genesis, this is chronologically before God gives him the sign of circumcision and before he offers up Isaac in the Aqedah. Yet this did not stop some intertestamental authors from asserting that God credited Abraham with righteousness on the basis of his future acts of obedience. We read in 1 Maccabees, 'Was not Abraham found faithful when tested, and it was reckoned to him as righteousness?'(1 Macc. 2.52). In other words some authors read Genesis 22 back into Genesis 15.

When Paul taps into the story of Abraham from the Scriptures, he is arguably critiquing competing ways of telling the Abraham story by both his fellow Jews (in Romans) and by his fellow Jewish Christians (in Galatians). At several points in Paul's letters, he evokes the example of Abraham in direct contrast to how he is being portrayed by his opponents.

In Romans, Paul can contrast the characteristics of fallen humanity who failed to give God glory (Rom. 1:23) with Abraham who did give glory to God (Rom. 4:20). For Paul, the Abrahamic narrative represents the beginning of the reversal of the fall and the undoing of Adam's transgression. Paul is not unique in that regard, for a rabbinic tractate states, 'I will make Adam first . . . and if he goes astray I will send Abraham to sort it out' (*Gen. Rab.* 14.6). In a similar fashion, Paul reads the Genesis narratives missi-ologically, as God's unfolding purposes for salvation are coming to fruition through Abraham and his seed. In Romans 9:7–8, Paul argues that not all of Abraham's physical descendants are members of Israel and not all of the true Israel is made up of Abraham's physical descendants.

In Romans 4, Paul uses the story of Abraham as proof from Scripture that God saves people by faith with the consequence that salvation is not by works and not limited to the people of Israel. Paul uses Genesis 15:6 and Psalm 32:2, linked by the catchword 'credit', to show that God credits righteousness based on faith, not on works of the law. This is as clear an attack on a work-for-reward theology of

merit as one can imagine. The 'works of the law' also include circumcision, and circumcision is one of the distinguishing marks of a
Jewish male. To say that God justifies only those who are circumcised would be to limit his salvation to the Jews. Since God justifies
apart from works of the law, circumcision or becoming Jewish is not
an essential part of being in a right relationship with him.

The proof of this point is Abraham, since he was credited with
righteousness prior to receiving circumcision. He received the sign
of circumcision as a 'seal' of the righteousness he already had by
faith and not as the condition upon which he received it. Thus,
Abraham is not the forerunner of proselytes (converts to Judaism
via circumcision) but is the forerunner of Christian Gentiles who
have faith in Christ.

So Abraham is the father of all who have faith, whether they are
circumcised or not. The promise made to him did not come
through the law, which brings wrath, but through faith, which
brings righteousness. Abraham had faith in God's life-giving
power and so do Christians when they confess the risen Lord. Paul
endeavours to draw a tangible connection between the *act* of
faith, the *object* of faith and the *result* of faith from Abraham to
his readers.[1] Paul carefully explains how Abraham received his
promises and blessings prior to being circumcised and prior to the
giving of the law itself.

In Galatians 3, Paul treats the Galatians' receipt of the Spirit as
equivalent to Abraham's receipt of righteousness. It is by believing
like Abraham that the Galatians become children of Abraham.
The promise to Abraham that he would be a blessing to the
nations is an anticipation of the gospel, since God justifies
Gentiles in the same way he justified Abraham: by faith. As in
Romans, and again in contrast to other Jewish interpretations of
Abraham that projected the law back into Abraham's lifetime, Paul
makes a contrast between Abraham and those who pursue works
of the law. The law does not bring the Spirit, sonship or righteousness, but curses for failing to obey it. In fact, Christ redeemed

---

1. M. F. Bird, *The Saving Righteousness of God: Studies in Paul, Justification, and the
New Perspective*, PBM (Milton Keynes: Paternoster, 2007), p. 50.

believers from this curse by becoming a curse for them so that they (Gentiles) might receive the blessings promised to Abraham, including the Spirit, who is the down payment of an inheritance in the world to come (Gal. 3:14; Eph. 1:13–14; Rom. 15:8).

The upshot is that you do not need to become a son of Moses in order to be a son of Abraham. The Mosaic covenant introduced 430 years after Abraham does not annul or abolish the promises given to Abraham. In this way, Paul is reading the Scriptures as a sequential narrative. Whereas the rabbis and their forebears could insist that in the Torah there is no before and after, Paul places Abraham in the wider context of redemptive history, where the promises made to Abraham are prior to the law and Mosaic covenant.

Furthermore, to make the inheritance dependent upon the law is to revoke the promise given to Abraham, a promise rooted in God's grace. While the law is not strictly opposed to the promises, it cannot bring those promises to reality, since law marks out sin as sin. Through faith and baptism, the Galatians are clothed with Christ and are part of the new creation that breaks down all ethnic barriers that arose out of the law. If they belong to Christ, then they are part of Abraham's seed and full heirs of the promise. Richard Hays puts it in these words:

> Paul wants to argue that Judaism itself, rightly understood, claims its relation to Abraham not by virtue of physical descent from him (*kata sarka*) but by virtue of sharing his trust in the God who made the promises. In that sense, the gospel, which invites all people, including Gentiles, into right relation with God through faith, confirms the Law; it is consistent with the real substance of the Law's teaching. This is the proposition that Paul sets out to demonstrate through his exposition of Genesis . . . the gospel confirms the Torah. Only a narrowly

Abrahamic Covenant

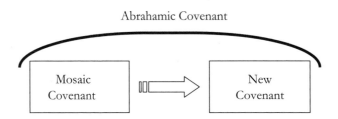

ethnocentric form of Judaism, Paul insists, would claim that God is the God of the Jews only or that Abraham is the progenitor of God's people 'according to the flesh,' that is, by virtue of natural descent.[2]

To follow that up, the figure above shows that Paul regards the covenant with Abraham as an overarching covenant that determines the role of the Mosaic covenant as a forerunner or precursor to the new covenant Jeremiah and Ezekiel foretold. The new covenant is the fulfilment of the Abrahamic covenant rather than simply the renewal or republication of the Mosaic covenant. Ben Witherington captures Paul's train of thought:

> The new covenant is but the consummation of the one begun with Abraham in ever so many ways: (1) The basis for obtaining the benefits of the Abrahamic and new covenant is faith in God's promises. (2) Both involve not only the circumcised but the uncircumcised. In Paul's view, circumcision is not seen as the essential thing that establishes the covenant with Abraham, for Genesis 15 precedes Genesis 17. (3) Both involve children given by God. (4) Both involve an everlasting covenant. (5) Both involve a promise of world, not merely of land, for *in* Abraham all the families of humankind were to be blessed, *from* Abraham were to come many nations (Gen. 17:6), and *through* his ultimate descendant — Christ, the seed of Abraham — they also become one family of God, both circumcised and uncircumcised. I thus conclude that in Paul's mind the new covenant in Christ is but the completion or fulfilment of the Abrahamic one.[3]

The story then goes: God called Abraham out of idolatry and God promised that through Abraham he would bless the nations. That was an anticipation of the gospel whereby the Gentiles receive the Spirit and sonship through faith in Christ, who is the promised seed of Abraham.

---

2. R. B. Hays, *Echoes of Scripture in the Letters of Paul* (New Haven: Yale University Press, 1989), pp. 54–55.

3. B. Witherington III, *Paul's Narrative Thought World* (Louisville: Westminster John Knox, 1994), p. 47.

Israel

The story of Israel is often retold in provocative and powerful fashion at several places in the Old Testament, such as
Deuteronomy 26:5 ('My Father was a wandering Aramean') and
Ezekiel 16:45 ('Your mother was a Hittite and your father an
Amorite'). The point of this retelling was to bring Israel's past
into proper perspective and so influence attitudes in the present.
Similarly, Paul has a renewed perspective on the story of Israel
in the light of the coming of Jesus. What defines Israel is no
longer ethnicity or Torah but spiritual sonship and being in the
Messiah.

Behind Galatians is the question 'Who are the people of God?'
or 'Who are the members of Israel?' For Paul the answer is, 'Those
who believe in the Messiah.' Yet the teachers who had begun
influencing the Galatians were urging them to take on law-
obedience to perfect what was lacking in Paul's message and to
complete their status in salvation. In Galatians 4:21–31, Paul presents an allegory which argues that the promises made to Abraham
are not necessarily mediated through the line of the law:[4]

Law	Christ
Abraham	
Hagar covenant	Sarah covenant
Ishmael ('flesh')	Isaac ('promise')
Persecutor	Persecuted
Children—slaves	Children—free
Mount Sinai	Mount Zion? Golgotha? Heaven?
Earthly Jerusalem	Heavenly Jerusalem
In slavery	In freedom
Proselytizers	Paul
Old covenant	New covenant

4. The diagram is taken from S. McKnight, *Galatians*, NIVAC (Grand
   Rapids: Zondervan, 1995), p. 229.

Paul has already argued in Galatians 3:15 – 4:7 that the law was an interim measure or parenthesis between the time of promise and fulfilment. The law was a *paidagōgos*, or guardian, to lead us to Christ. Here in Galatians 4, Paul puts forward a creative argument (perhaps echoing similar arguments used by the Galatian intruders) that the promises do not automatically accumulate through adherence to the law or by being a member of national Israel. Instead, the promises come through a different line altogether: that of *faith*. It is unsurprising that at the end of Galatians Paul offers a benediction upon the 'Israel of God' (Gal. 6:16). Commentators disagree whether this means ethnic Israel, Jewish Christians who do not oppose Paul, or the church as the union of Jews and Gentiles.

I prefer the last option for three reasons:

1. Paul has just spent a whole letter arguing for the unity of Jews and Gentiles in one body, so it is highly unlikely he now at the end of the letter splits up Jews and Gentiles and includes only Jews under the privileged title the 'Israel of God'.
2. Paul elsewhere uses language ordinarily used to describe Israel to designate Christians (e.g. Phil. 3:3; Col. 3:12).
3. Paul is unlikely to issue a blessing upon Israel irrespective of whether or not they believe in Christ, since those who do not love Christ are under a curse (1 Cor. 16:22).

In 2 Corinthians 3, Paul contrasts two covenants and two ministries: that of Moses and that of Christ and the apostles. The Mosaic covenant was robed in splendour and glory, but that glory faded and brought death. In contrast, the new covenant has an even greater and surpassing glory that brings life. Paul contrasts the effect of the law on human beings with the effect of the Spirit: the letter kills but the Spirit gives life; the Mosaic covenant brings condemnation but the new covenant brings righteousness.

Romans deals with the question of Israel and reading Israel's history in the light of the coming of Jesus. In chapter 2, Paul engages in a fictitious debate with a Jewish opponent. The overarching premise is that God's impartiality means that the Jew has no grounds for boasting before God. He cannot, due to his hypocrisy, appeal to a moral superiority based on *performance* of Torah (2:1–11). Likewise, he cannot, due to the existence of (Christian) Gentiles who fulfil Torah in a manner superior to many Jews, appeal to his *possession* of Torah (2:12–16).

Neither can national privilege (2:17–24) nor the badge of circumcision (2:25–29) establish a claim before God for justification. Paul mentions the divine calling of Israel to be 'guides to the blind' and a 'light to those in the darkness', a theme found elsewhere in Jewish literature.[5] He builds on the Scriptures which say that Israel was called to be a 'kingdom of priests' (Exod. 19:5–6) and 'a light to the nations' (Isa. 42:6; 49:6). An Israel that refuses to be Israel *for the sake of the world* accordingly forfeits its covenantal position. Israel's problem is failing to keep the righteousness of Torah and refusing to live up to the covenantal mandate to extend God's salvation to the nations.

Instead, they boast in their obedience to Torah and their election over and against the nations. But they forget that circumcision is only of value if one has obedience, and obedience can be reckoned as good as circumcision (you can see where Paul is going with this and he paves the way for what he will say in Rom. 9). Lest Paul be misunderstood, in Romans 3:1–5 he affirms the advantage and privilege of the Jewish people, the proviso being that they affirm the impartiality of God when it comes to meting out justice.

Paul in many ways returns to these themes in Romans 9 – 11 in order to deal with the question of 'Israel' in greater depth. In this section, he fights a battle on two fronts. The first is against Gentiles who might be tempted to think that the gospel is for the Gentiles instead of Israel. The second is against Jews, Jewish Christians and proselytes who suppose that God's provision for salvation remains organically cocooned around Israel. Paul begins in Romans 9 with an impassioned wish for self-anathematization on behalf of Israel. He then lists the blessings of the Jewish nation. After this comes his reflection on Israel in three distinct

---

5. Cf. *Sib. Or.* 3.194–195; *T. Levi* 14.4; Josephus, *Apion* 2.291–295.

phases: (1) Israel in the past (9:6–29), (2) Israel in the present (9:30 – 10:21), and (3) Israel in the future (11:1–36).[6]

In terms of the past, the existence of a remnant of faithful believers is nothing new and is attributable exclusively to God's electing grace. In the present, Israel's zeal for Torah makes them stumble over Christ. Tragically, they have rejected the one who brings the law to its appointed goal so there would be righteousness for all who believe (Rom. 10:4). The impartiality of God implies the culpability of Israel for her ignorance, but also marks the widening of the horizon of salvation in admitting Gentiles into the hope of Israel due to Israel's failure to believe.

As for the future, the example of Israel's failure comes as a warning to Gentiles. If God can cut off the natural branches of an olive tree (Israel), he can also cut off the branches unnaturally grafted in (Gentiles). Yet with the warning comes a promise. The flip side is that if God can graft in the unnatural branches to the olive tree (Gentiles), how much more can he graft in branches natural to that same olive tree (Israel). The covenant faithfulness of God means he will never wipe his hands of Israel once and for all. Paul's hope is that the influx of Gentiles will prompt Israel to jealousy and to receive her Messiah, so that, at the end, 'all Israel will be saved' (Rom. 11:26).

Jesus

The story of Jesus holds immeasurable significance for Paul. First, the incarnation is referred to at several points through the 'sending' of Jesus (Gal. 4:4; Rom. 8:3) and the pattern of Jesus' humiliation and exaltation in the light of his pre-existence (2 Cor. 8:9; Phil. 2:5–11). Second, the obedience and faithfulness of Jesus are also important for Paul. Milton's epic poem *Paradise Regained* is not set on the cross, but in the temptation narratives, as it is through Jesus' obedience to the Father in the face of temptation that salvation is won.

---

6. T. H. Tobin, *Paul's Rhetoric in its Contexts: The Argument of Romans* (Peabody: Hendrickson, 2004), p. 321.

There is no question that Paul regards the obedience of Jesus as having a saving effect in Romans 5:12–21, but I am also convinced that in at least two places Paul refers to the saving value of Jesus' own faithfulness, namely Ephesians 3:12 and Philippians 3:9 (see the NET). For instance, I would translate Philippians 3:8–9 as follows:

> For his sake I have suffered the loss of all things, and I regard them as human filth, in order that I may gain Messiah and be found in him, not having a righteousness of my own that comes from the Law, but one that comes through the *faithfulness of the Messiah*, the righteousness from God based upon faith.

We can note that the correlation between Jesus' obedience and God's saving action implies that what Christ did and what God did are two sides of the same coin.[7]

A more subtle question is whether or not Paul had any knowledge of the 'historical Jesus'.[8] Over a generation ago much was made of 2 Corinthians 5:16, where Paul refuses to know 'Christ according to the flesh'. This was garnered as evidence of the apostle's deliberate lack of interest in the historical figure of Jesus. On the contrary, Paul states that he formerly viewed Christ from a worldly perspective but now comprehends him from the vantage of one who is 'in Christ'. Paul may be referring to his former knowledge of Christ, which operated with a false notion of messiahship, or else acknowledging his prior hostility towards the Jesus movement. On either account, there can be no deprecating of Paul's interest in the historical Jesus. Jerome Murphy-O'Connor writes:

> The historical Jesus is fundamental to Paul's theology. The disciple who wrote Ephesians caught the Apostle's approach perfectly when he

---

7. L. E. Keck, 'Paul in New Testament Theology: Some Preliminary Remarks', in *The Nature of New Testament Theology*, ed. C. Rowland and C. Tuckett (Oxford: Blackwell, 2006), p. 114.

8. Cf. M. F. Bird, 'The Purpose and Preservation of the Jesus Tradition: Moderate Evidence for a Conserving Force in its Transmission', *BBR* 15 (2005), pp. 164–165.

presents Jesus as the truth of Christ (Eph. 4:21). When his converts attempted to separate the Christ of faith from the Jesus of history, Paul resisted by insisting that the Lord of Glory was the crucified Jesus (1 Cor. 2:6), and by stressing that Christ had been received 'as Jesus the Lord' (Col. 2:6). The implication that Paul had preached the historical Jesus is formally confirmed by his condemnation of anyone 'who preaches a Jesus other than the one we preached' (2 Cor. 11:4).[9]

In Paul's letters, the Jesus tradition occurs in one of two forms, either in direct *citation* of Jesus' words or in passages that *echo* Jesus' teaching.[10] Notably, these citations/echoes of Jesus' teachings occur more frequently in sections that discuss practical matters (e.g. 1 Cor. 7 – 15; Rom. 12 – 15; Col. 3; 1 Thess. 5).

To give a few examples, in 1 Corinthians 7:10–11, Paul presents Jesus' prohibition on divorce (Mark 10:9–12; Matt. 5:31–32; 19:3–9; Luke 16:18). The command in 1 Corinthians 9:14 to allow those who preach the gospel to make a living out of the gospel is an allusion to the words of Jesus in Luke's missionary discourse (Luke 10:7). The Lord's Supper tradition contained in 1 Corinthians 11:23–25 recalls the words of Jesus at the Last Supper (Mark 14:22–25; Matt. 26:26–29; Luke 22:14–23). On the whole, Paul's employment of the Jesus tradition is best described as a 're-presentation' rather than as a quotation.[11] As to what Paul says about Jesus in his letters (and this may not represent the sum of his knowledge) we observe the following:

> He was born as a human (Rom. 9:5) to a woman and under the law, that
> is, as a Jew (Gal. 4:4), that he was descended from David's line (Rom. 1:3;
> 15:12); although he was not like Adam (Rom. 5:15), that he had brothers,
> including one named James (1 Cor. 9:5; Gal. 1:19), that he had a meal on

9. J. Murphy-O'Connor, *Paul: A Critical Life* (Oxford: Oxford University Press, 1997), p. 91.

10. See D. Wenham, *Paul: Follower of Jesus or Founder of Christianity?* (Grand Rapids: Eerdmans, 1995).

11. S. Kim, 'Jesus, Sayings of', in *DPL*, ed. G. F. Hawthorne, R. P. Martin and D. G. Reid (Downers Grove and Leicester: IVP, 1993), p. 482.

the night he was betrayed (1 Cor. 11:23–25), that he was crucified and
died on a cross (Phil. 2:8; 1 Cor. 1:23; 8:11; 15:3; Rom. 4:25; 5:6, 8;
1 Thess. 2:15; 4:14, etc.), was buried (1 Cor. 15:4), and was raised three
days later (1 Cor. 15:4; Rom. 4:25; 8:34; 1 Thess. 4:14, etc.), and that
afterwards he was seen by Peter, the disciples and others (1 Cor. 15:5–7).[12]

A crucial point to take away is that in Paul's letters there is no indication that he played off the 'Christ of Faith' against the 'Jesus of
History'. The fulcrum of his Christology is the identification of
the crucified Jesus with the risen and exalted Lord.

The church

A final story we must consider is that of the church. Paul's letters
inform us of the life and struggles of many of the churches in
Palestine, Syria, Asia Minor, Greece, Italy and Crete. This group
goes by many names: the *ekklēsia*, or church, the body of Christ,
the saints, the beloved and the elect. They are a worshipping
community, a cosmopolitan community, a teaching community, a
Spirit-led community and a missional community. They are new
creations (2 Cor. 5:17) and no longer find privilege or status in
economic, social, gender or ethnic distinctions but in Christ
Jesus, who unites them (Gal. 3:28; 5:6; 6:15; 1 Cor. 7:19; Col.
3:11).

In this sphere, there is 'one Lord, one faith and one baptism'
(Eph. 4:5). In the church, persons are enjoined in a single table-
fellowship, worshipping the same Lord, partakers of the one
Spirit, having a shared faith, united by the bonds of baptism,
reaching out in a common mission, and pursuing the things that
make for peace and mutual encouragement. That is not to say that
everything was perfect for these churches. They suffered persecution and struggled to find some kind of solidarity with local Jewish

12. S. E. Porter, 'Images of Christ in Paul's letters', in *Images of Christ: Ancient
and Modern*, ed. S. E. Porter, M. A. Hayes and D. Tombs (Sheffield:
Sheffield Academic Press, 1997), pp. 98–99.

communities. Amid all this there were also internal divisions, which at times became quite vitriolic, as 1 and 2 Corinthians demonstrate.

In Romans 14 – 15, we find Paul's recipe for how persons of different convictions can live together in worshipful harmony. Paul constantly had to admonish believers to live an upright ethical life in a pagan world where morality was often disengaged from religion, or else the indigenous religions promoted sinful practices. At the same time, Paul took solace from the fact that God was at work in these people to bring his purposes to fruition (Phil. 2:12–13) and was conforming them to the image of his Son (e.g. Rom. 8:29; 12:2; 2 Cor. 3:18). In the end, it would be the faithfulness of God that would ensure his apostolic ministry had not been in vain (1 Cor. 1:8–9).

The *ekklēsia*, then, is the people of God, called to be the new Israel and the renewed humanity (e.g. Col. 3:1–17). The church was to be charismatic (Spirit-endowed), multi-ethnic (Jew and Gentile), Christocentric (Lord's Supper, baptism and imitation of Christ), unified (baptized into one body), part of society (mission) but not a reflection of it (holiness).

4. READING SOMEONE ELSE'S MAIL

As we have already said, Paul is best known through his letters. When we read these letters, it is like reading someone else's mail.[1] Paul's letters were written *for* us but not *to* us. So when we read them, we are entering into a conversation but only hearing the one side of that conversation. What follows is a basic summary of each letter in the Pauline corpus, highlighting its background, content and significance.[2]

I consider this an important chapter to include because I have found that many Christians and even many senior undergraduate students simply do not know what each letter is about. Being able to quote the odd inspiring verse from Romans by memory or knowing the history of Pauline scholarship like the back of your

---

1. R. B. Hays, *First Corinthians* (Louisville: Westminster John Knox, 1997), p. 1.

2. For more extended summaries of each letter see I. H. Marshall, *New Testament Theology: One Gospel, Many Witnesses* (Leicester: Apollos, 2004); and C. L. Blomberg, *From Pentecost to Patmos* (Nottingham: Apollos, 2006).

hand is useless unless you also know what Paul actually says in his letters and what each letter is roughly about. That is why I urge my students to learn the outlines to each book of the New Testament and to have a basic grasp of the terrain Paul covers in each letter. Which is what I hope this chapter achieves.

Galatians: contending for the truth of the gospel

Sometime before the Jerusalem council (see Acts 15), Paul learned that agitators had arrived in Galatia and were urging his converts there to be circumcised and to follow the law of Moses. These intruders were essentially benign in their criticism of Paul and probably saw themselves as adding to what was apparently lacking in Paul's message and explaining that Paul's omission of circumcision was due to his duplicity on the matter.

Paul's opening greeting emphasizes the divine origin of his apostleship and the cosmic power of Christ's death that delivers believers from sin and the evil age. Notably, there is no thanksgiving for the Galatians: Paul is unhappy (1:1–5). He embarks on an ironic rebuke of the Galatians for so quickly turning to another gospel, and by launching this tirade against them proves he is not a 'man-pleaser' as some allege (1:6–10). In what follows, Paul narrates his conversion experience and emphasizes at length that he received his gospel by direct revelation from Christ and that it was not mediated to him through the Judean church leaders (1:11–24).

Paul writes how he made another visit to Jerusalem, taking Titus with him, and not only was Titus not compelled to be circumcised but James, Cephas (Peter) and John recognized the validity of Paul's gospel and the legitimacy of his apostolate to the Gentiles (2:1–10). Yet when Cephas came to Antioch he withdrew from joint Jew–Gentile fellowship at the behest of 'certain men from James' who took exception to the practice of allowing Gentiles to attend fellowship meals as equals without first becoming proselytes to Judaism. Paul embarks on a stirring rebuke of Peter's hypocrisy (given his earlier behaviour in Acts 10 – 11), and says that his actions are not 'walking towards the truth of the gospel' (2:11–14).

In the succeeding verses, we find Paul laying out his central

thesis for the letter: justification by faith without works of the law
(2:15–21). He then argues that it is receipt of the Spirit and not
submission to the law that makes the Galatians sons of Abraham
(3:1–5). Paul shows the conformity of his gospel to the scriptural
pattern by demonstrating from Genesis 15:6 and Habakkuk
2:4 that righteousness comes through faith, in contrast to
Deuteronomy 27:26 and Leviticus 18:5, which show that the law
brings curses not righteousness and life (3:6–14).

Next, Paul shows that the coming of the Mosaic law does not
abrogate or nullify the promises made to Abraham, as the law was a
temporary custodian until the promised seed of Abraham came
(3:14–29). The work of Christ brings believers into the inheritance
of sonship, not slavery (4:1–7). To take on the law after receiving
salvation in Christ is tantamount to returning to the form of slavery
from which they were originally delivered (4:8–20). The allegory of
Hagar and Sarah proves that going back to the Mosaic covenant is
to submit to slavery, when they are in fact already children of the
free woman (4:21–31). Instead, the Galatians should rejoice in their
freedom and not undergo circumcision (5:1–12). This freedom,
however, brings obligations. So the Galatians are to live life according to the Spirit and not according to the flesh (5:13–26).

Paul then includes some final instruction for life in the community (6:1–10) and closes with an impassioned plea that the
Galatians not let themselves be circumcised, because the work of
the cross is superior to the work of circumcision (6:11–18). The
crux of Galatians is the uncompromising centrality of the gospel
as well as its sufficiency for salvation and its transforming power
for living the Christian life.

1–2 Thessalonians: an ending worth waiting for

After his period of ministry in Thessalonica, Paul moved on to
Athens and Corinth, where he then wrote to the Thessalonians to
encourage them in the face of adversity and to quicken their
enthusiasm for the parousia (1 Thessalonians), and then again to
clarify any misunderstandings or misrepresentations made about
the parousia (2 Thessalonians).

In 1 Thessalonians, Paul's opening greeting includes reference to his co-workers Silas and Timothy, and he makes known his prayer of thanksgiving for the Thessalonians' faith, love and hope in Jesus (1:1–3). Paul was a model to them just as they have become a model of perseverance to all the churches of Macedonia and Achaia (1:4–10). Paul reminds the Thessalonians of his behaviour among them: he was hardworking, God-honouring and never self-seeking (2:1–12). Paul in turn offers additional thanks for them, especially in the face of Jewish opposition (2:13–16), and says he longs to see them (2:17–20). The details of the sending and return of Timothy, who informed Paul of the Thessalonians' situation, climaxes in a short prayer on their behalf (3:1–13).

Paul next offers an exhortation for them to live a God-pleasing life. This means avoiding sexual impurity, pursuing brotherly love and living a quiet and productive life before outsiders (4:1–12). It appears that some of the Thessalonians have problems with the parousia, particularly the fate of believers who have died or will die prior to the event. Paul's answer is that when the Lord returns, the deceased believers will be raised first and the remaining believers will be transformed immediately, words that should encourage the Thessalonians (4:13–18). However, the exact time is unknown and the believers should live appropriately in the light of the Lord's coming (5:1–11). Paul closes with some general exhortations and the grace (5:12–28).

In 2 Thessalonians, Paul begins with a salutation from himself, Silas and Timothy, and thanksgiving for the Thessalonians (1:1–4). Paul notes their suffering and says that God will repay those who afflict them (1:5–10), and he prays for them that God will be glorified in their perseverance (1:11–12). Paul continues by assuring the Thessalonians that they have no cause for alarm due to purported prophecies, teachings and letters that say the 'Day of the Lord' has already come. (2:1–2). Paul reasons that the 'Day' will not appear until rebellion comes first and the man of lawlessness is revealed (2:3–12). As such, he urges them to remain steadfast to the traditions they have received and he offers a prayer on their behalf (2:13–17). Likewise, Paul asks them to pray for him and his co-workers and reminds them of God's faithfulness to them (3:1–5). That is followed with a warning against idleness and disobedience to his instructions (3:6–15). The letter closes with a benediction and Paul's autograph (3:16–17).

1–2 Corinthians: the good, the bad and the Corinthians

After Paul established a church in Corinth during his Aegean mission, he left and returned to Ephesus via Antioch and Jerusalem. In the interim, Apollos, and probably Peter, had visited Corinth, resulting in the development of certain factions there. Paul wrote a previous letter to the Corinthians (see 1 Cor. 5:9) urging them not to associate with sexually immoral people who profess to be brothers. Paul heard reports from Chloe's household about various divisions and quarrels (1 Cor. 1:11) and also received three delegates from Corinth – Stephanas, Fortunatus and Achaicus (16:17) – who brought him a gift, further information and questions from the Corinthians about certain matters.

1 Corinthians begins with Paul's greeting from himself and Sosthenes (1:1–3) and his thanksgiving for the spiritual enrichment of the Corinthians by God (1:4–9). Paul then attends to the matter of internal divisions and partisanship based around key personalities (1:10 – 4:21). He emphasizes that the cross abolishes all pretensions to power and status, all ministers of the gospel will have their labours judged and greatness is to be found in humiliation and service as exemplified by the apostles.

In 5:1 – 6:19, Paul deals with reports about unseemly behaviour among the Corinthians, including a man who is coupled with his stepmother, lawsuits among believers, and an exhortation to flee sexual immorality of all kinds. From 7:1 to 16:11 Paul responds to several questions and reports. He touches on questions about celibacy, singleness, divorce and marriage (7:1–40), and food sacrificed to idols (8:1–13). He provides a defence of his apostleship against those who question his motives concerning the collection of money, and presents his discipline and self-denial as proofs of his apostleship (9:1–27).

This leads into a discussion of the history of Israel in the wilderness as a semi-climax to the discussion: those who do not persevere, those who commit idolatry and all the sexually immoral will experience judgment (10:1–13); they are to refrain from participation in cultic pagan meals (10:14–22); and meat purchased from the market can be eaten on the condition that it does not cause a brother to stumble (10:23 – 11:1). The subsequent material covers problems related to communal gatherings, including the issue of women and head coverings (11:2–16), abuses related to the Lord's Supper (11:17–34), and disputes revolving around spiritual gifts and order in worship (12:1 – 14:40).

Paul then engages with the view that there will be no future resurrection by advocating that resurrection is integral to the gospel of the early church, Jesus' resurrection is the prototype of a future resurrection body and the future body will be both continuous and discontinuous from their present state of existence (15:1–58). Paul gives instruction concerning the collection (16:1–4), intimates his future travel plans, including his intention to send Timothy, and urges support for the leadership of Stephanas (16:5–18). Paul closes with his final greeting, a blessing and his autograph.

Between 1 and 2 Corinthians, Timothy arrived in Corinth and found that the situation had deteriorated and was more than he could handle. After hearing of this, Paul then proceeded on a 'painful visit' to Corinth, resulting in a heated confrontation between Paul and several others. We do not know when or exactly why Paul soon left, but, to make matters worse, some itinerant 'apostles' with letters of commendation arrived in Corinth and were inflaming the situation by calling into question Paul's apostolic credentials (2 Cor. 3:1–5; 11:13–15).

Paul then wrote the Corinthians a third letter out of his great distress, which affirmed his love for them and called them to obedience in all things (2 Cor. 2:3–9; 7:8–13). The letter called for the ringleaders opposing Paul to be dealt with and was delivered by Titus, who was able to report back to Paul that the rift had been healed.

2 Corinthians commences with a short salutation and an extended thanksgiving (1:1–11). Paul then defends his travel itinerary, since he wishes to avoid any further confrontation with the Corinthians (1:12 – 2:4). He gives instructions for how the person who opposed him is to be restored to the Corinthian community (2:5–11). Following this, Paul narrates the events leading up to the current letter, including his recent evangelistic work. He pleads the

purity of his motives and maintains that for such work he needs no letter of commendation, since the Corinthians are themselves his letter of commendation (2:12 – 3:3). Paul's confidence stems from the fact that he is a minister of the glorious new covenant, which is superior to the old covenant (3:4–18).

With such an important charge, Paul affirms his commitment to the integrity of this ministry even when it is discharged under harrowing and crushing circumstances, but he is able to carry on through God's renewing strength (4:1–18). Although Paul and his co-workers are wasting away in the light of their hardship, they also know that if their mortal bodies are destroyed, they will put on a heavenly dwelling. They press on, knowing they will give an account of their ministry before God (5:1–10). Paul describes his ministry as one of persuasion and reconciliation as an ambassador for Christ (5:11–21).

Based on this, the Corinthians are urged not to receive God's grace in vain (6:1–2). Because of such hardships, the Corinthians should receive him as he receives them (6:3–13). Paul offers a further admonition against fraternizing with pagans and exhorts them to pursue purity and holiness (6:14 – 7:1). Paul returns to the topic of his relations with the Corinthians and expresses his joy at the news Titus has brought him (7:2–16). He then urges them concerning the collection for the impoverished saints in Jerusalem (8:1 – 9:15).

2 Corinthians 10 – 13 may seem somewhat disjointed from what precedes it (some argue it is an interpolation from one of Paul's 'other' letters), but Paul is probably trying to pick up a few loose ends concerning the legacy of the 'super-apostles' who were in Corinth and may have tried to solicit funds from the Corinthians. That would have hampered Paul's own collection for the Jerusalem poor. There, Paul provides a concerted defence of his apostolic ministry (10:1–18) and responds to the false apostles as being little more than charlatans who do not stand up to the test of the true marks of an apostle (11:1–33). While Paul may boast in his weakness, it is this weakness that ironically displays God's great power through him (12:1–10). Paul explains his plan for a third visit and hopes that there will be no need for further confrontation (12:11 – 13:10). He closes with a final greeting and a trinitarian benediction (13:11–14).

Philippians: surprised by joy, fazed by finances

Paul writes to the Philippians from prison (probably Rome, but possibly Caesarea or Ephesus), and the letter pours forth thanksgiving, joy and encouragement. Paul commends the Philippians for their giving, while also seeking further material support from them.

The letter opens with greetings from Paul and Timothy and is addressed to the saints, deacons and overseers of the church, which is followed by Paul's thanksgiving and prayer for the Philippians (1:1–11). Paul narrates how his imprisonment has served the advancement of the gospel by encouraging others to speak the word more boldly (1:12–18) and looks forward to being set free in answer to the Philippians' prayers (1:19–26). Paul urges them to live a life worthy of the gospel in the face of opposition (1:27–30). There are exhortations towards unity (2:1–4) and Paul urges the Philippians to follow the example of Christ in humility in a beautiful hymn about the incarnation (2:5–11).

That is followed by further exhortations for obedience and holiness in a corrupt environment (2:12–18), and Paul outlines the plans for Timothy and eventually for himself to visit them (2:19–24). Paul then notes that he will send back to them Epaphroditus, one of their number, who has suffered a grave illness (2:25–30). Paul gives a stern warning about those who advocate circumcision. This is probably based on his prior skirmishes with those of the circumcision group elsewhere rather than because of the presence of Jewish-Christian proselytizers in Philippi, for which we have no evidence (3:1–11). Paul enjoins the Philippians to imitate him and press on towards the goal rather than follow the enemies of the 'cross', should they appear on the scene (3:12 – 4:1).

Paul then offers some miscellaneous comments on unity among certain women and on rearing godly virtues and behaviours (4:2–9). He next takes up what is his primary concern, from his position at least, in that he is thankful for their generosity towards him, with the underlying expectation that they will again contribute to his needs (4:10–20). The letter finishes with a greeting from the saints in Caesar's household and the grace (4:21–23).

Colossians: the sufficiency and supremacy of Christ

Colossians is another captivity epistle (a letter composed while Paul was in prison), written possibly from Rome in the early 60s, although one should not too quickly discount an Ephesian provenance. The epistle was part of two circular letters Paul sent to the churches of the Lycus valley in central Asia Minor (churches he had not personally established or visited), the other letter being sent to the Laodiceans (4:16). In Colossians, Paul is countering the claims of Jewish Hellenists or Jewish mystics who are propagating Judaism in Colosse by using language drawn from religious beliefs indigenous to the Lycus valley.

After the opening greeting, Paul gives his customary thanksgiving, which here centres on the faith and love of the Colossians and God's act of rescuing them from darkness and transferring them into the kingdom of his Son (1:1–14). After this, Paul sets forth a majestic Christ hymn that establishes the central thesis of his letter, namely the sufficiency and supremacy of Christ in creation, salvation and over all principalities and powers (1:15–20). As an encouragement to them, Paul follows this up with reference to Christ's reconciling work (1:21–23) and the afflictions Paul himself has suffered in his ministry (1:24 – 2:5).

In language reminiscent of Galatians, Paul urges the Colossians not to pay heed to the 'deceptive philosophy' that consists of circumcision, observing Jewish festivals, angel-centred mysticism, and ascetic practices (2:6–23). This is because the Colossians have died and been raised with Christ and are constituted as the new Israel and the new humanity. As such, they are commanded to put to death certain behaviours, and to cultivate certain godly virtues as a consequence (3:1–17).

Paul gives directions for the running of Christian households in relation to husbands and wives, parents and children, as well as slaves and masters (3:17 – 4:1), and the manner in which Christians should relate to outsiders (4:2–6). His final remarks refer to Tychicus, who will inform them of Paul's situation, greetings from Paul's companions, an encouraging word for Archippus, and a short benediction (4:7–18).

Philemon: salvation and slavery

The letter to Philemon was occasioned by the flight of Onesimus, Philemon's slave, to Paul. Written from Rome, or possibly Ephesus, Paul urges Philemon to forgive Onesimus and to receive him back not as a runaway slave but as a repentant brother in Christ.

The letter opening greets Philemon, Apphia, who is probably Philemon's wife, and Archippus, who is probably the pastor or elder of the house church in Colosse (1–3). Paul then offers an exuberant prayer of thanksgiving for Philemon, specifically for his faith and love (4–7).

Next Paul makes an impassioned plea on the basis of love for Onesimus, who became his 'son' (converted) during Paul's imprisonment (8–11). Paul feels obliged to return Onesimus to Philemon, although he wishes that the new convert could stay and lend assistance to him in the gospel. Paul hopes this will occasion reconciliation between the two if Philemon receives him back, not merely as a slave but as a brother (12–16). Paul pleads with Philemon to welcome Onesimus, offers to repay Philemon for any debt and is confident that Philemon will do as asked due to his debt to Paul (17–21). Paul makes a request, probably rhetorical, that a guest room be prepared for him for a future visit (22). The letter closes with greetings from Paul's co-workers and with the words of grace (23–25).

Ephesians: the majesty and mystery of Christ

This letter, closely resembling Colossians, was written by Paul from Rome and was probably intended as a circular letter. The letter is not refuting any particular heresy or deviant behaviour but is an exercise in worshipful instruction. The goal as such is to praise the glory of God and of Christ and to enrich the faith of the audience through an extended meditation on God's glory.

Beyond the opening greeting is a lavish and highly poetic section of praise to God for his mercy and grace. This section also includes the central motif of Ephesians, namely the revelation of the mystery of God's will set forth in Christ, who executes the Father's design to bring harmony to the chaotic universe (1:1–14). This is followed with thanksgiving and a prayer for the letter's recipients (1:15–23). Paul then moves on to remind his audience of salvation by grace through faith (2:1–10), which in turn leads to a section on the membership of Jews and Gentiles in one body (2:11 – 3:6). Paul draws attention to his role as a minister of the gospel, the gospel which states that God's ancient purposes are worked out in Jesus Christ (3:7–13).

That in turn leads Paul to a moment of prayer for spiritual renewal, and closes with a doxology of praise (3:14–21). Subsequent attention is given to the importance of unity anchored in one faith, one Lord, one baptism, one God and Father of all as well as in the ministries of apostles, prophets, evangelists and pastor-teachers who build up the body of Christ (4:1–16). The accompanying exhortation prescribes how believers are to walk before God in a pagan world (4:17 – 5:21) and how Christian households are to be configured concerning relations between wives and husbands, children and parents, and slaves and masters (5:22 – 6:9). Paul follows this up with an exhortation to put on the armour of God (6:10–20). The letter closes with a reference to Tychicus, who will inform them of Paul's situation, and with a benediction (6:21–24).

Romans: pursuing the things that make for peace

Romans was written from Corinth around AD 55–56 and was composed in order to secure support from the churches in Rome for Paul's planned mission to Spain. Towards that end Paul provides an overview of his perspective on salvation, the law, righteousness, ethics and Israel. The epistle also serves to prevent the church in Rome from fragmenting along ethnic lines in the aftermath of the exile and return of Jewish Christians from Rome during the reigns of Claudius and Nero. In brief, the purpose of Paul in this epistle is to 'gospelize' the Romans: to conform them to the power and reality of the gospel (Rom. 1 – 8), to help the Gentile Christians understand how they relate to the unbelieving Jewish world

(Rom. 9 – 11), to urge them to live out the values of Jesus Christ in the Greco-Roman world (Rom. 12 – 13) and to exhort them to live in worshipful harmony with a Jewish-Christian minority (Rom. 14 – 15).[3]

Paul's opening greeting makes particular reference to his gospel of the Lord Jesus Christ, from whom Paul received grace and apostleship with the task of bringing Gentiles to the obedience of faith (1:1–7). Paul offers his customary thanksgiving and outlines his hope to one day travel to Rome (1:8–15). After this, he sets forth the central thesis of the letter, the revelation of the righteousness of God in the gospel, which is received by faith (1:16–17).

Paul highlights the ongoing revelation of God's wrath against every form of human wickedness and rebellion (1:18–32). He then changes tack, and in a dialogue with an imaginary Jewish opponent describes the failings of the Jewish people. Paul refutes the view that Jewish boasting in Torah or in election will result in their acquittal on the Day of Judgment (2:1 – 3:8). Consequently, all people, Jews and Gentiles, are helpless in sin and have no hope for vindication before God (3:9–20). This tragic state of affairs is reversed by the manifestation of the righteousness of God in Jesus Christ's death, which through redemption, atonement and justification delivers Jews and Gentiles from sin. This is apprehended by faith and not by works and so proves that neither religious effort nor ethnicity is of any inherent value in salvation (3:21–31).

Paul uses the example of Abraham to reiterate the point that justification is by faith without works, so that Gentiles can be part of God's family as Gentiles without having to come via the route of conversion to Judaism (4:1–25). Paul then begins to admix themes of assurance, as he overtures the ethical imperatives created by justification, introduces the imagery of reconciliation and reflects on the magnitude of divine grace (5:1–11). The

3. M. F. Bird, *The Saving Righteousness of God: Studies in Paul, Justification, and the New Perspective*, PBM (Milton Keynes: Paternoster, 2007), p. 141 (see pp. 140–152 for an expanded introduction to Romans).

Adam/Christ typology clarifies the widened scope of salvation, so that justification creates not only a worldwide Abrahamic family, but also a renewed humanity. Believers shift from the epoch of sin, death and condemnation associated with Adam's transgression to the epoch of righteousness, life and justification associated with the obedience of the New Adam (5:12–21).

Paul anticipates several objections to his teaching. If the law is not a means to attaining righteousness, and if law no longer marks out the people of God, then it is legitimate to ask, 'What is the motivation for righteous behaviour and what was the point of giving the law in the first place?' Paul's exhortation to righteousness is predicated on one crucial premise: the transforming power of the gospel and the new obedience created by union with Christ. Christ is the sphere of holiness, righteousness and redemption, and all those in Christ are emancipated from the old age of sin and death, and are uniquely empowered by their baptism into Christ to live their lives in complete service to God (6:1–23).

The purpose of the law was to mark out sin as sin; but law has no power to effect either redemption or transformation. In that sense, Torah points to salvation but does not provide it (7:1–25). The subsequent section encapsulates a kaleidoscope of themes and arguments about the power of God's saving righteousness, the outworking of righteousness in the life of the believer through the Spirit, the vindication of God's people at the final assize, and the insurmountable assurance that Christians have (8:1–39).

The reference to assurance leads naturally into a discussion concerning Israel (chs. 9–11), since their failure to believe in the Messiah potentially casts aspersions on God's faithfulness. Beyond Paul's impassioned wish for self-anathematization on behalf of Israel and his listing of the blessings of Israel comes his reflection on Israel in the past, the present and for the future.[4] God's election of Israel means that Israel's 'no' to Jesus will eventually turn into a 'yes' when the Messiah returns again to Zion. Paul then sets out a blueprint for life in the Christian community: sacrificial service

---

4. T. H. Tobin, *Paul's Rhetoric in Its Contexts: The Argument of Romans* (Peabody: Hendrickson, 2004), p. 321.

to God (12:1–2) and the exercise of spiritual gifts and offices
(12:3–8).

He also outlines the character of Christian ethics (12:9–21). The
ethics of Christians should benefit the fabric of society and
Christians should respect governing authorities (13:1–7). While
free from the law, Christians are not free from the law of love
(13:8–10) and are to live under adverse circumstances knowing
that the day of salvation is near (13:11–14).

Paul then engages divisive issues pertaining to food and fellowship. Echoing teaching from 1 Corinthians 8, he instructs his
audience to exercise their convictions and freedoms in a loving
way in order to build each other up and for the 'strong' to receive
the 'weak' (Rom. 14:1 – 15:13). The conclusion of the letter intimates Paul's travel plans to Jerusalem and Spain (15:14–33). Paul
commends Phoebe the carrier of the letter (16:1–2), offers a long
list of greetings to persons he knows (16:3–16), makes a final
warning about divisive persons, adds a personal note about his co-
workers and closes with a doxology (16:17–27).

Pastorals: faithful sayings for faithful friends

The Pastoral Epistles were, assuming Pauline authorship,[5] written
towards the end of Paul's life when he was in prison in Rome. The

---

5. In scholarly literature, it is disputed whether Paul did in fact write several
   of the letters attributed to him. The authenticity of 2 Thessalonians,
   Colossians, Ephesians and the Pastoral Epistles are all questioned. The
   three letters that comprise the Pastoral Epistles in particular are said to
   have very strong arguments against the likelihood that Paul authored
   them. The arguments for this are that (1) there are some difficulties in
   accommodating the Pastorals to a chronology of Paul's life; (2) the
   epistolary format of the Pastorals varies somewhat from Paul's other
   letters; (3) the degree to which the vocabulary and grammar of the Greek
   reflects Paul's own literary style is debated; (4) the picture of Paul that
   emerges from the Pastorals is said to look somewhat like a hero of the
   faith from a previous generation; and (5) some of the theological

letters have as their destination Timothy in Ephesus and Titus in Crete. We are justified in treating these letters as a distinct body (the Pastoral Epistles) given a common string of 'faithful' or 'trustworthy' sayings (1 Tim. 1:15; 3:1; 4:9; 2 Tim. 2:11; Tit. 3:8), the references to the *epiphaneia* (appearing) of Jesus (1 Tim. 6:14; 2 Tim. 1:10; 4:1; Tit. 2:13), and the pastoral instructions for Paul's co-workers that occur across all three letters. At the same time, we should not ignore the distinctive context, occasion and theology of each letter.[6]

1 Timothy commences with a salutation to Timothy (1:1–2) and immediately launches into an attack on false teachers who promote myths rather than God's work (1:3–11). Paul then testifies to the mercy and grace that saved him and strengthened him over the course of his ministry (1:12–17) and gives some encouraging words to Timothy to fight the good fight of the faith (1:18–20). Paul asks that prayers be given for those in authority (2:1–7) and provides instructions on the dress and conduct of women in the congregation (2:8–15). That is followed up with a list of qualifications for overseers and deacons (3:1–13) and an exhortation about Christian households (3:14–15). We find after that a short hymn or creed about the incarnation, which encapsulates the theology of the Pastorals (3:16).

There is an additional warning about the false teachers who promote ascetic practices (4:1–5). In contrast, Timothy is to be a faithful servant and to carry out his ministry diligently (4:6–16). Paul then begins a large section about community relations between men and women of all ages, about widows, advice for the

---

concepts and expressions like 'righteousness' and 'faith' seem to have a different orbit of meaning compared to usage of the same terms in the undisputed letters. Alternatively, the letters are highly personalized and it remains entirely feasible that an amanuensis or secretary such as Luke had a freer hand in the composition of these letters and perhaps even completed them on Paul's behalf shortly after his death so that his co-workers could still receive encouragement from the apostle. See recently in favour of Pauline authorship, P. H. Towner, *The Letters of Timothy and Titus*, NICNT (Grand Rapids: Eerdmans, 2006), pp. 83–89.

6. Ibid., pp. 67–68.

elders, for Timothy himself, and remarks on slaves (5:1 – 6:2). Paul
warns once more about the false teachers, this time in relation to
money (6:3–10), and commands Timothy to flee from such things
and to cultivate certain virtues as he defends the faith (6:11–16).
Paul tells Timothy to order the rich not to place too much value in
wealth. Paul closes the letter with a final exhortation to Timothy to
guard what has been entrusted to him (6:17–21).

2 Timothy begins with a similar greeting (1:1–2) and Paul offers
encouragement to Timothy to fan into flame the gift of God he
received (1:3–7). Paul asks Timothy not to be ashamed of him,
because Paul is not ashamed of the gospel (1:8–14). Paul narrates
his circumstances, including a mixture of desertion and dedication
by those around him (1:15–18). He urges Timothy to be strong in
God's grace and to transmit his teachings to others (2:1–7). Paul
then rehearses the essential message of the gospel, which climaxes
in a short hymn or creed (2:8–13). In contrast to the false teachers,
Timothy is admonished to be a competent workman who handles
the Word of truth responsibly (2:14–26). Paul explains that the last
days will be characterized by wickedness and apostasy (3:1–9).

Paul is grateful that God has constantly rescued him from all of
his travails (3:10–13), and admonishes Timothy to remain true to
the Scriptures that equip him for his good work (3:14–16).
Timothy is then encouraged to be a constant and faithful preacher
of the word, who commits himself to evangelism (4:1–5). The
nearness of Paul's death becomes apparent when he refers to his
own life being poured out like a drink offering as he awaits the
crown of righteousness (4:6–8). Paul makes some personal
remarks about several individuals and the circumstances concerning his various trials (4:9–18), and ends the letter with a final
greeting and the grace (4:19–22).

Titus opens with a longer-than-average greeting about the hope
of eternal life that has appeared through the preaching of the apostles (1:1–4). Paul explains that he left Titus in Crete in order to
straighten things out and to appoint elders with the appropriate
qualifications (1:5–9). Paul warns Titus of the rebellious people
of the circumcision group in Crete (1:10–16). Paul gives further
instruction on what must be taught to certain persons such as older
men, older women, young men and slaves (2:1–10). The coming of

salvation means that all believers are to live holy lives as they await the glorious appearing of Jesus Christ (2:11–15). The Christians in Crete are to obey their rulers and authorities and do good to all (3:1–8). Paul tells Titus to avoid foolish controversies about the law and to warn divisive persons (3:9–11). The letter closes with instructions about several individuals, final greetings and the grace (3:12–15).

5. THE ROYAL ANNOUNCEMENT

Some gospel presentations go like this:

1. God is holy.
2. Man is sinful.
3. The only way sinful man can stand before a holy God is if there is a mediator who stands in our place to remove our sin and is obedient to God in our stead.
4. The gospel declares to us that Jesus has perfectly fulfilled the law of God and his death has atoned for sins.
5. Therefore, through faith in Jesus our sins are cancelled and his obedient life is counted as ours, so we can be at peace with a holy God.

The gospel is not an inference made from a deductive argument about God's holiness and human sin. Such an approach is not so much wrong as it is deficient. Instead, the gospel is the story of Jesus the Messiah, his death and resurrection, and faith and repentance towards him. There are several potential errors that follow if we articulate the gospel as a series of linear propositions in need of resolution rather than seeing it as the fulfilment of a redemptive-historical story.

First, sometimes it is assumed that what God really requires is X number of frequent-flyer points in order to fly persons from hell to heaven. Yet because of our sinful and wretched state, we have no frequent-flyer points of our own. But Jesus has earned plenty himself and has put his frequent-flyer points in our account so that we can go to heaven when we die. While it is true that Jesus' obedience and faithfulness genuinely effect our salvation, this approach makes God out to be some kind of cosmic accountant who needs the ledger to be balanced before he can open the doors to Paradise.

In contrast, I suggest that Jesus' obedience is important not because he earns the frequent-flyer points we do not have, but because he is the *new Adam* and the *true Israel* who is obedient where humanity and Israel failed to be. Jesus succeeds where Adam and Israel floundered. Jesus enters into the cycle of suffering and punishment as one who is not guilty of disobedience or transgression and, therefore, is vindicated as righteous and enabled to transfigure humanity and reconstitute the new Israel in his own person. His faithfulness and obedience become ours when, through faith, we are united to his person and so partake of his righteousness, share in his vindication and join in his triumph over death and sin.

Second, all that some approaches require of Jesus is a sinless birth and a sin-bearing death. The actual content of his life matters little and pales into insignificance when compared to his death. On this perspective, Jesus' life has the sole purpose of acquiring the necessary merit for salvation to ensue, and his teachings are construed to show people how to be good Christians and how to get to heaven. If that is the case, then it is scarcely possible to make sense of the Gospels when Jesus says, 'I was sent only to the lost sheep of the house Israel' (Matt. 15:24), or when Paul says that 'For I say to you that Christ has become a servant of the circumcised on behalf of God's truth, to confirm the promises made to the Fathers' (Rom. 15:8).

How does Jesus' mission to Israel slot into God's purpose in redemptive history? Was Jesus' mission to Israel a bottleneck that had to be traversed before the real mission of proclaiming Jesus to Gentiles got under way? Alternatively, the story of Jesus as the fulfilment of God's plan for Israel is a fundamental presupposition for Paul's gospel proclamation. Jesus is not only *from* Israel, as if it were a matter of historical convenience, but is *for* Israel as well. Israel's covenant charter was to extend salvation to the ends of the earth, and Jesus makes that charge a reality.

For Paul, it is Jesus' mission to Israel that enables Gentiles to participate in the promises made to the patriarchs (Rom. 15:8). Christ was cursed on the cross not merely so that sinners could go to heaven, but so that the blessings of Abraham might come to the Gentiles (Gal. 3:13–14). Israel had a prominent place in redemptive history by being the chief recipients of the promises made to the patriarchs and by being the agents through whom the Messiah would come into the world.

That is why Paul takes great pride in being a Jew: he knows that the Messiah came through the Jews, and will save both Jews and Gentiles (Rom. 9:5; 11:25–26). Israel's law as covenant charter is not a bad thing that has been done away with, but is a good thing that finds its resolution and climax in Christ, so there can be right-eousness for everyone without distinction (Rom. 10:1–13). In Luke's account of Paul's speech in Pisidian Antioch, Paul says, 'We tell you the good news: What God promised to our fathers he has fulfilled for us, their children, by raising up Jesus' (Acts 13:32–33). The gospel means the validation of Israel's special place in God's plan and is the divine 'yes' to God's promises to Israel, promises related to blessings and descendants. The gospel story is how Jesus fulfils the Law and the Prophets and brings the Gentiles into salva-tion and into the widening family of Abraham.

Third, in contrast to some gospel presentations, the resurrec-tion and parousia should not be regarded as an afterthought to the gospel. In some descriptions of the gospel, the resurrection becomes merely the proof that Jesus died for our sins, which, though true, falls short of the full riches of the saving significance of the resurrection. Paul states that forgiveness of sins is tied to the resurrection (1 Cor. 15:17) and even justification (Rom. 4:25). Similarly, the parousia or return of Christ is not an embarrassing epilogue to a story well and truly finished when we get to heaven, but it marks the arrival of the new heavens and the new earth and consummates God's purposes for creation. To use the language of

Ernst Käsemann, the parousia is the moment where God finally repossesses the world for himself.

Fourth, we should recognize the Jewish and Greco-Roman context of the gospel and its roots in the Jesus tradition. In Isaiah 40:9–11 and 52:7–10,[1] the good news is that God will not allow Israel to languish in the mire of exile, but will gather the exiles in a new exodus so that there is mercy and redemption for Israel. God himself will come like a shepherd to feed and nurture his people and reign among them. Jesus himself proclaimed a gospel clearly linked to the Isaianic hopes for restoration (Luke 4:18–21; Luke 7:18–23/Matt. 11:2–6) and this comports with messianic hopes traceable in the Dead Sea Scrolls (4Q521 2.8–14). Mark's summary of Jesus' message is that he preached the 'gospel of God' and the coming 'kingdom of God' (Mark 1:14–15). Jesus' correlation of 'gospel' and 'kingdom' makes the dynamic saving reign of God spoken about in the Prophets the object of faith.

What is more, it is an announcement that the long-awaited day for God to become king is now a burgeoning reality, as evidenced by his healings, exorcisms and miracles. In the first century, a 'gospel' could also refer to the good news of the birth, coming of age or accession of the Roman emperor and the inauguration of a new world order with peace and prosperity for the empire. So when Paul says 'gospel', he is echoing hopes from Israel's sacred traditions. He is also continuing Jesus' own proclamation in a post-Easter context by saying things that might make Greeks or Romans think he was announcing a king who rivalled Caesar.

The gospel as story

There is undoubtedly an inner logic about the gospel, but the gospel at its core is a story that has Christ as the centrepiece. The gospel, then, is the climactic scene in the stories of God and God's Son. Some might object that this fascination with narrative theology is simply an offshoot of postmodernity that eschews

---

1. And similarly in other literature like *Pss. Sol.* 11.

logic in favour of story. Not so. Consider this quote from Martin Luther:

> The gospel is a story about Christ, God's and David's Son, who died and was raised and is established as Lord. This is the gospel in a nutshell . . . And I assure you, if a person fails to grasp this understanding of the gospel, he will never be able to be illuminated in the Scripture nor will he receive the right foundation.[2]

Martin Luther was evidently doing narrative theology four hundred years before it was even fashionable! Thus, we should seek to get inside the story of the gospel and to exposit the full theological significance of this story and what it tells us about God, human beings and salvation. What I want to do below is look at a few texts from Paul and see what they have to say about the gospel.

1 Corinthians 15:1–5

> Now I want you to know, brothers and sisters, that the gospel that I preached among you, which you in turn received, in which you also stand, through which you are also being saved, if you hold firmly to the word that I proclaimed to you — unless you have come to believe in vain. For what I received I delivered to you as of first importance:
>
> that Christ died for our sins
> according to the Scriptures,
>   and that he was buried,
>   and that he was raised on the third day
> according to the Scriptures,
>   and that he appeared to Cephas, then to the twelve.

The gospel as set out here has several constituent elements.
1. *Christ died and was raised.* The most basic Christian belief was

---

2. M. Luther, 'A Brief Instruction on what to Look for and Expect in the Gospels', in *Luther's Works*, ed. J. Pelikan and H. T. Lehmann, 55 vols. (St. Louis: Concordia; Fortress: Philadelphia, 1955–86), vol. 35, pp. 118–119.

that Jesus died and rose (e.g. 1 Thess. 4:14; 2 Cor. 5:15; Rom. 4:25). That Christ 'died' is an obvious reference to his crucifixion, while 'raised' is a divine passive and implies that Jesus was raised *by God*. Furthermore, it means that the primary content of the gospel is the death and resurrection of Christ and that this dual event has inherent saving significance.

2. *Christ died 'for our sins'*. The idea here is probably a reflection of the Greek text of Isaiah 53:5–6, 11–12, where the Suffering Servant bears the transgressions, sins and iniquities of Israel as their representative. Paul does not set forth an explicit theory of atonement here (such as penal substitution), since he is more interested in the *effects* than the *mechanics* of Jesus' death and resurrection,[3] but there is the operating assumption that what alienates people from God is sin, and the death of Christ removes that sin and enables humans to have fellowship with God again. At the same time, we have no reason to think Paul means anything different from what he says elsewhere about Christ being a sacrifice or ransom who dies in our place (Rom. 3:22–25; 5:6, 8; 14:15; 2 Cor. 5:14–15, 21; Gal. 1:4; 2:20; 3:13; 1 Thess. 5:9–10; 1 Tim. 2:6). The preposition *hyper* (for) usually means 'for advantage of', but it would be an odd thought to think our sins are advantaged by or benefit from Christ's death.

More likely, Christ's death affects sins by removing them or atoning for them. Christ's death for our sins means that he takes the consequences of our sins.[4] In addition, the expression 'for our sins' (*hyper tōn hamartōn hēmōn*) is probably analogous to 'sin offering' (*peri hamartias*), as in the Septuagint, the second-century BC Greek translation of the Old Testament (e.g. Lev. 5:11; 7:37; see Rom. 8:3), highlighting the sacrificial dimension to Christ's death. What is more, there are cases where the preposition *hyper* overlaps with *anti* (in place of), as in Romans 9:3, 1 Corinthians 15:29 and 2 Corinthians 5:15, again suggesting that substitution lies in the

---

3. S. McKnight, *Jesus and His Death: Historiography, the Historical Jesus, and Atonement Theory* (Waco: Baylor University Press, 2005), p. 347, n. 44.

4. S. Gathercole, 'The Cross and Substitutionary Atonement', *SBET* 21 (2003), pp. 160–161.

background here.[5] We should also note that in 1 Corinthians 15:17, Paul maintains that without the resurrection there is no forgiveness of sins. The forgiveness of sins, then, requires both Jesus' death and his resurrection.

3. *This act is 'according to the Scriptures'*. Paul does not tell us which Scriptures and how they relate to the gospel. He probably has in mind Scripture as a unified whole, as seen in the light of Christ. The Aqedah, exodus, Passover, sacrificial system and Suffering Servant all foreshadow the saving nature of Christ's death, and several of the psalms, such as 16:8–11 and 110:1–4, point forward to the resurrection of David's son. The main point is that the story of Christ's death and resurrection lines up with the Scriptures, so that Christ's work is neither entirely unprecedented nor wildly innovative. The gospel is a continuation and fulfilment of God's dealings with Israel.[6] Furthermore, it indicates that Christ's death and resurrection were predetermined and necessary in the divine plan (see also Luke 24:25–27, 44–46; and Acts 8:35).

4. *The gospel is what saves*. The death and resurrection of Christ are the objective grounds of salvation: they testify to what God did on behalf of humans. The gospel is also the content of what is believed. Paul tells the Corinthians that this gospel is what they received, what they take their stand on, and they will be saved if they hold to it. Salvation comes through believing that Jesus died and was raised in accordance with the Scriptures.

5. *The gospel is not a Pauline innovation*. This is because it is part of the pattern of material he received from Greek-speaking Jewish Christians (probably in Damascus or Antioch). In verse 11, Paul states this gospel is what the other apostles have also preached. Paul endorses the tradition that proclaims the death and resurrection of Christ and interprets it in terms of the saving and transforming power of God that receives

5. D. B. Wallace, *Greek Grammar Beyond the Basics* (Grand Rapids: Zondervan, 1996), pp. 383–389.

6. R. B. Hays, *First Corinthians* (Louisville: Westminster John Knox, 1997), p. 255.

explanation and intelligibility within the framework the Jewish Scriptures provide.[7]

Romans 1:1–4 and 2 Timothy 2:8

> Paul, a servant of Jesus Christ, called to be an apostle, set apart for the gospel of God, which he promised beforehand through his prophets in the holy Scriptures:
>
> > the gospel concerning his Son,
> > who was born from the seed of David
> > according to the flesh
> > and was designated the Son of God in power
> > according to the Spirit of holiness
> > by resurrection from the dead,
> > Jesus Christ our Lord.

Similar to 1 Corinthians 15:3–5, there is a reference to Jesus' resurrection and the fulfilment of what God promised in the Prophets and holy Scriptures. Yet, whereas 1 Corinthians 15:3–5 focuses on the *work* of Christ as the key ingredient of the gospel, Romans 1:3–5 centres on the *identity* of Jesus Christ as the content of the gospel. At the fore of the gospel is Jesus' role as the Son of David, Son of God (Messiah) and Lord. Paul emphasizes the prophetic and public announcement that Jesus is the promised Messiah and sovereign Lord, the gospel in a nutshell. Which is why elsewhere Paul can refer to the 'gospel of Christ' (cf. Rom. 16:25; 1 Cor. 9:12; 2 Cor. 4:4; 9:13; Gal. 1:7; Phil. 1:27; 1 Thess. 3:2): the content is the person.

But notice how Paul prefaces his formula with the designation 'gospel of God' (cf. Rom. 15:16; 1 Thess. 2:2, 8–9; 1 Tim. 1:11). While the gospel has Christ as its primary contents, it must be set in relation to the God of Israel. The gospel of Christ is also the gospel of God. In other words, to tell a story about the identity and work of Christ is ultimately to make a statement about God and his dealings with the

---

7. A. C. Thiselton, *The First Epistle to the Corinthians*, NIGTC (Grand Rapids: Eerdmans, 2000), pp. 1184–1185.

world through his Son. The resurrection is singularly significant here, since it 'designated' Jesus as the Son of God. The word *horizō* can mean 'declare' or 'appoint', but it should not be used in support of an adoptionist Christology whereby Jesus only became the Son at his *resurrection*; more likely, the resurrection transformed Jesus' sonship into a new eschatological function he did not previously discharge.[8] Additionally, the phrase 'from/by resurrection from the dead' (*ex anastaseōs nekrōn*) also marks out Jesus' resurrection as the beginning of the general resurrection (cf. Acts 4:2; 23:6; 1 Cor. 15:20, 23; Col. 1:18; Rev. 1:5). The gospel must then be placed in apocalyptic coordinates, since Jesus' death rescues believers from the old age (Gal. 1:4) and his resurrection marks the entrance of the new age (Rom. 1:4).

It is worth adding here 2 Timothy 2:8, which is much like Romans 1:3–4. There, Paul says, 'Remember Jesus Christ, raised from the dead, from the seed of David – according to my gospel.' The similarities are Jesus' Davidic lineage (Messiahship) and his resurrection. Placed side by side, Romans 1:3–4 and 2 Timothy 2:8 show that proclaiming the gospel means heralding that Jesus reigns. He is the locus of God's salvation and lordship, the goal of the prophetic promises, his resurrection ushers in the new age, and he will execute the divine prerogative of judgment on the appointed day (cf. Acts 17:31; Rom. 2:16; 14:10; 2 Cor. 5:10; 2 Tim. 4:1). As Tom Wright says of Paul's gospel, 'His announcement was that the crucified Jesus of Nazareth had been raised from the dead; that he was thereby proved to be Israel's Messiah; that he was thereby installed as Lord of the world. Or, to put it yet more compactly: Jesus, the crucified and risen Messiah, is Lord.'[9]

Now we must get the balance correct here. We should not itemize the gospel as a huge list of things one must believe in order to be saved, such as the imputation of Christ's righteousness, the pre-tribulation rapture, biblical inerrancy or the substance of the sacraments. Yet, 1 Corinthians 15:3–5 clearly makes belief in the saving power of Jesus' death and resurrection necessary

---

8. See further D. J. Moo, *The Epistle to the Romans*, NICNT (Grand Rapids: Eerdmans, 1996), pp. 48–49.

9. N. T. Wright, *What Saint Paul Really Said* (Oxford: Lion, 1997), p. 46.

for salvation: the gospel is what one believes in and is saved by.

On the other hand, we have to acknowledge that the gospel includes a proclamation of the kingship and reign of the Lord Jesus Christ. The gospel is an explosive announcement that the despised and rejected one is now installed in a place of authority and deserves the acclaim normally reserved only for the greatest of worldly kings, for the highest gods of the pantheon, and even for the covenant God, Yahweh. In other words, Jesus is king and reigns over all.

But merely stating that Jesus is king is an insufficient representation of the gospel if we do not point out how he has shown his kingly power in giving himself up for our sins and being raised by God for our acquittal.[10] The gospel is a royal announcement that God has become king in Jesus Christ and has expressed his saving sovereignty through the death and resurrection of the Son, which atones, justifies and reconciles. There is no gospel without the heralding of the king, and there is no gospel without atonement and resurrection.

Taken together, we can infer from 1 Corinthians 15:3–5, Romans 1:1–4 and 2 Timothy 2:8 that the gospel is about both the person and work of Christ. God promised in the Scriptures that he would renew creation and restore Israel. The gospel is the good news that God has made these promises good in Jesus, the Messiah and Lord. Jesus died and rose for the purpose of atoning for sins and through faith in him and his work believers are reconciled to God. The new age has been launched and God has revealed his saving righteousness in the gospel so that he justifies and delivers persons from the penalty and power of sin and death.

The gospel and Caesar

Imagine it is the late 1930s and you are in a lavish hotel in Berlin for a sumptuous dinner with a cohort of German industrialists,

---

10. This is my criticism of N. T. Wright, who wants to reduce 'gospel' to the proclamation that Jesus is Lord. See his 'Romans', in *New Interpreters Bible*, ed. L. E. Keck, 12 vols. (Abingdon: Nashville, 2002), vol. 10, pp. 416–419, and esp. n. 30 against D. J. Moo; Wright, *Saint Paul*, p. 45.

bankers, barons, university lecturers and officers from a German SS Panzer division. The evening is relatively cheerful and the mood jovial; conversation revolves around the weather, advice on financial investments, holiday plans in Austria and the latest operas. Then an SS officer taps his glass and proposes a toast to the Führer, Adolf Hitler, to his health and the new Germany, and everyone raises their glasses. And then you, being the committed Christian you are, propose another toast and bellow out in your best German, 'Jesus ist Führer!' Now what manner of reaction do you suppose it would prompt from those SS officers? Do you think they would even entertain the idea that Germany has room for two Führers, the other being a Jew?

In the ancient world, the title 'Lord' (*Kyrios*) was also used of the Roman emperor. In the Roman era, terms like grace, gospel, *parousia*, justice, freedom, Lord, Saviour and Son of God were employed in Roman political propaganda and utilized in the prayers and rites of the imperial cult, which focused on worship of the Roman emperor. By analogy, then, the 'good news' that 'Jesus is Lord' carried with it the implication that Caesar was *not* Lord. Jesus is the vice-regent of the God of Israel and brooks no rivals. We see that Paul's gospel had theopolitical consequences in that it claimed for Jesus an immense authority and power which threatened that of Rome.

In the early first century of the common era, the fastest-growing religion in the eastern Mediterranean was the imperial cult. Cities like Ephesus and Pergamum competed for the right to be the official wardens of that cult. Exuberant temples for the cult were constructed in places like Pisidian Antioch, Corinth, Philippi, and even in Palestine. Some emperors took their divinity more seriously than others, though. Augustus, for instance, forbade emperor worship in Italy, while Caligula demanded it. The imperial cult was a means of uniting the diverse smelting pot of tribes and peoples Rome had subjugated. It promoted loyalty, unity, social cohesion, patronage and political stability around the emperor and the empire.

Roman citizens in all provinces were expected to participate in the cult of Rome, while non-citizens were expected to pay their respects to Rome and Augustus. At the same time, the cult was not simply imposed on unwilling recipients but was gratefully welcomed and promoted, as cities wanted the security of Roman protection, and various guilds and associations coveted the patronage of the emperor. The imperial cult permeated every aspect of Greco-Roman society, including parades, dinner parties, festivals, religious rituals, citizenship, athletic games and gladiatorial contests, which all bore the stamp of the Roman state religion.[11] Stephen Price writes:

> The cult was a major part of the web of power that formed the fabric of society. The imperial cult stabilized the religious order of the world. The system of ritual was carefully structured; the symbolism evoked a picture of the relationship between the emperor and the gods. The ritual was also structuring; it imposed a definition of the world. The imperial cult, along with politics and diplomacy, constructed the reality of the Roman empire.[12]

It was Virgil who wrote that the emperor Augustus was 'a god who wrought for us this peace – for a god he shall ever be to me; often shall a tender lamb from our folds stain his altar' (*Ec.* 1.6–8).[13] While Horace, who made an art out of poetic brown-nosing, said this of Augustus: 'Thunder in heaven confirms our faith – Jove rules there; but here on earth Augustus shall be hailed as god also, when he makes new subjects of the Britons and the dour Parthians' (*Odes* 3.5). The Roman emperors demanded of their subjects absolute allegiance, as illustrated by the oath the people of Aritium swore to the new emperor, Gaius Caligula, upon his accession in AD 37:

> On my conscience, I shall be an enemy of those persons whom I know to be enemies of Gaius Caesar Germanicus, and if anyone imperils or shall imperil him or his safety by arms or by civil war I shall not cease to hunt him down by land and by sea, until he pays the penalty to Caesar in full. I shall not hold myself or my children dearer than his safety and I shall consider as my enemies those persons who are hostile to him. If

---

11. M. J. Gorman, *Apostle of the Crucified Lord: A Theological Introduction to Paul and His Letters* (Grand Rapids: Eerdmans, 2004), pp. 16–17.

12. S. R. F. Price, *Rituals and Power: The Roman Imperial Cult in Asia Minor* (Cambridge: Cambridge University Press, 1984), p. 248.

13. All citations of classical authors are from the Loeb Classical Library, Harvard University Press.

consciously I swear falsely or am proved false may Jupiter Optimus
Maximus and the deified Augustus and all the other immortal gods
punish me and my children with loss of country, safety, and all
my fortune.[14]

This was the world in which Paul proclaimed his gospel that 'Jesus
is Lord'. Importantly, the counter-imperial surge of Paul's message
is not for the sake of being fashionably rebellious. Paul is no
idealistic iconoclast in his early twenties naively imitating the anti-
government ravings of his liberal arts college professors. When
Paul spits in Caesar's direction, it is because the things of Caesar
stand opposed to the purposes of God.

Most important of all, we should note carefully that Paul takes
such a dangerous stance as part of the pastoral care of his converts. As Ben Witherington states:

> He is no armchair theologian pondering out the meaning of theological
> minutiae. He is, rather, doing his best pastorally to shore up the beliefs
> and behaviour of his converts so that they can endure as part of a
> countercultural movement under pressure and persecution. He
> deliberately draws on imperial rhetoric in his theological expressions and
> transferring it to Christ and the Lawless One [2 Thess. 2:8–9] because he
> believes that only Jesus is truly Lord and that the emperor has no right to
> command absolute allegiance, much less worship.[15]

Let us look briefly, then, at some of the parallels between the
terminology of Paul's gospel with its Old Testament background
and the imperial cult.[16]

---

14. Cited from J. R. Harrison, 'Paul and the Imperial Gospel at Thessaloniki',
   JSNT 25 (2002), p. 80.
15. B. Witherington III, *1 and 2 Thessalonians: A Socio-Rhetorical Commentary*
   (Grand Rapids: Eerdmans, 2006), p. 237.
16. This table is adapted from Gorman, *Apostle of the Crucified Lord*,
   pp. 108–109; and the examples are cited from C. A. Evans, *Mark 8:27–16:20*,
   WBC (Nashville: Thomas Nelson, 2001), pp. lxxxi–xciii; and *LANE*, pp. 338–378.

Terms	Old Testament background	Greco-Roman meaning	Example of Greco-Roman meaning
euangelion (gospel)	Good news that Yahweh is revealing his saving reign to deliver Israel.	Good news of military victory or the birth, triumph, accession or benefaction of the emperor.	'But the birthday of the god was the beginning of the good news, on his account, for the world' (inscription). When news spread of Vespasian's accession to the throne, 'every city celebrated the good news and offered sacrifices on his behalf' (Josephus, *War* 4.618). 'On reaching Alexandria Vespasian was greeted by the good news from Rome and by embassies of congratulations from every quarter of the world, now his own . . . The whole empire being now secured and the Roman state saved beyond expectation' (Josephus, *War* 4.656–657).
kyrios (Lord)	Translation of the Hebrew tetragrammaton for Yahweh, the God of covenant and creation.	Imperial title for the master of the Greco-Roman world, or used to designate pagan gods.	'Nero, the lord of the whole world' (inscription). 'Emperor [Augustus] Caesar, god and lord' (inscription). 'Vespasian the lord' (P.Oxy 246).
parousia (presence)	Presence of God.	Imperial or official visit of the emperor to a city or province.	'The sixty-ninth year of the first *parousia* of the god Hadrian in Greece' (inscription). Requisition of corn for the visit of king Ptolemy 'and applying ourselves diligently, both day and night, unto fulfilling that which was set before us and the provision of 80 artabae which was imposed

Terms	Old Testament background	Greco-Roman meaning	Example of Greco-Roman meaning
			for the *parousia* of the king' (from the wrappings of a mummified sacred crocodile in Egypt, 2nd century BC).
sōtēr (saviour)	God as deliverer, rescuer or redeemer of Israel.	The emperor as the one who ends civil wars, gives sustenance during famine and protects the empire against the Germanic tribes in the north and Parthians in the east.	In an inscription in Ephesus, Julius Caesar is described as 'the manifested god from Ares and Aphrodite and universal saviour of human life'. 'Emperor Caesar Augustus, saviour and benefactor' (inscription). 'Nero Claudius Caesar . . . saviour and benefactor of the inhabited world' (inscription).

I am not trying to make Paul out to be some kind of political dissident who spent a vast amount of time orchestrating the downfall of the Roman Empire. A cursory glance at Romans 13:1–7 shows that the apostle instructed Christians to submit to governing authorities because they are instituted by God and promote public order. But Paul did not know of a neat separation between church and state and did not think faith in Jesus meant having a purely interiorized spirituality. The gospel of Paul was deeply subversive, and even menacing, in the eyes of the Roman authorities, which is precisely why they persecuted Christians. Nero did not throw Christians to the lions because they confessed that 'Jesus is Lord of my heart'. It was rather because they confessed that 'Jesus is Lord of all', meaning that Jesus was Lord even over the realm Caesar claimed as his domain of absolute authority. It was unthinkable to the Roman political apparatus that the god of a subjected territory (Yahweh) and a Jew crucified in Judea on charges of insurrection (Jesus) were being afforded devotion, worship and faith, while rites to Caesar were neglected or denounced by these followers of Christ. Paul's gospel should be situated in terms of the clash of the gods of Rome and the God of Israel. Tom Wright describes Paul's ministry like this:

> His missionary work . . . must be conceived not simply in terms of a travelling evangelist offering people a new religious experience, but of an ambassador for a king-in-waiting, establishing cells of people loyal to this new king, and ordering their lives according to his story, his symbols, and his praxis, and their minds according to his truth. This could only be construed as deeply counter-imperial, as subversive to the whole edifice of the Roman Empire; and there is in fact plenty of evidence that Paul intended it to be so construed, and that when he ended up in prison as a result of his work he took it as a sign that he had been doing his job properly.[17]

In this context, to proclaim a 'gospel' where a victim of Roman violence was 'Lord' and 'Saviour' was an act of treason. Several texts from early Christianity illustrate this further.

First, Luke narrates that Paul's ministry in Thessalonica resulted in riots, where some believers were violently seized and brought before the authorities and accused of 'acting contrary to the decrees of the emperor, saying that there is another king named Jesus' (Acts 17:7). It is apparent that Christ and Caesar represent mutual exclusives in the minds of the Thessalonian authorities.

Second, in the post-apostolic era the refusal by Christians to worship Caesar resulted in notorious persecutions and martyrdoms. In the *Martyrdom of Polycarp*, a Roman official asks Polycarp, 'What evil is there in saying, "Caesar is Lord" and offering sacrifice with the associated ceremonies and saving yourself?' But Polycarp refused to comply and went to his death in the arena (*Mart. Pol.* 8.2).

Third, in the *Martyrdom of Paul*, Nero finds out his servant Patroclus has been revived from the dead and greets him:

---

17. N. T. Wright, 'Paul's Gospel and Caesar's Empire',
   <http://www.ctinquiry.org/publications/wright.htm>, accessed 4 April 2007.

But when he came in and saw Patroclus he cried out, 'Patroclus, are you alive?' He answered, 'I am alive, Caesar.' But he said, 'Who is he who made you alive?' And the boy, uplifted by the confidence of faith, said, 'Christ Jesus, the king of the ages.' The emperor asked in dismay, 'Is he to be king of ages and destroy all kingdoms?' Patroclus said to him, 'Yes, he destroys all kingdoms under heaven, and he alone shall remain in all eternity, and there will be no kingdom which escapes him.' And he struck his face and cried out, 'Patroclus, are you also fighting for that king?' He answered, 'Yes, my lord and Caesar, for he has raised me from the dead.' And Barsabas Justus the flat-footed and Urion the Cappadocian and Festus of Galatia, the chief men of Nero, said, 'And we, too, fight for him, the king of the ages.' After having tortured those men whom he used to love he imprisoned them and ordered that the soldiers of the great king be sought, and he issued an edict that all Christians and soldiers of Christ that were found should be executed.

(*Acts of Paul* 11.2)

The author of this apocryphal story about Paul (writing sometime in the late second or early third century) clearly thought that the kingdom of Christ stood over and against the kingdom of Caesar, and that Roman persecution of Christians was motivated by that observation. He may have been creative in his story-telling, but his knowledge of Christian–imperial relations was surely on the mark.

Conclusion

I once read in a *Trivial Pursuit* question that Charlie Chaplin entered a Charlie Chaplin lookalike contest and came second! By analogy many Christians cannot recognize a counterfeit gospel when they encounter it. As a result many tolerate short pithy one-liners in its place, like 'God loves you and has a wonderful plan for your life', which is a poor substitute for the real gospel. Paul does not want Christians duped by a pseudo-gospel of 'Jesus plus the latest Fad', nor does he want the gospel reduced to touchy-feely psychobabble. Paul's estimation of the human condition is that we need a Saviour, not a therapist.

The centre of Paul's gospel is the death and resurrection of

Jesus Christ, the Lord and Messiah. The death and resurrection of Christ is 'for us' or 'for' salvation. This gospel is articulated in such a way as to line up with the hopes contained in Israel's Scriptures that God would become king and restore the fortunes of Israel. The gospel also possesses an eschatological singularity that sets it over and against the good news of the imperial cult. The gospel of Christ is the announcement that God's saving power exerted in Jesus Christ brings to realization God's plan for Israel and for humanity: life, hope, peace and joy. As such, Paul's gospel is related to the stories of creation and of Israel, and sets forth Paul's view of God's rescue plan to renew creation through the salvation that comes through Israel's Messiah. Paul's gospel is also related to a number of other theological concepts such as the forgiveness of sins, the righteousness of God, reconciliation and justification. These concepts explicate the salvation brought by the gospel and will be examined in the next chapter.

6. THE *CRUX* OF THE GOSPEL

I remember hearing the story of an American evangelist who, as part of his evangelistic strategy, would go up to people in airports rather confrontationally and ask them, 'When did you get saved?' The assumption being that they were not really 'saved' and he would then tell them how to become so. On one particular day, he went up to a man and asked him this stock standard question, 'When did you get saved?' The man was startled by such an abrupt approach and responded by saying, 'Two thousand years ago, but I only found out about it recently.' The evangelist wanted to know when the man had made a decision or confession of faith, but the man responded by referring to the objective grounds of salvation, namely the cross and resurrection of Jesus Christ.

The cross and resurrection of Jesus dominate Paul's gospel proclamation and also comprise the centre of his theological thought. The foundation upon which his theological reflection is built is that salvation comes through the death and resurrection of Christ. They are the *crux* of the gospel, and all he says about salvation flows from his explanation of their significance. Paul has a repertoire of metaphors, expressions, images and concepts that explicate what the cross and resurrection actually achieve. Jesus' death and resurrection are the coherent centre of Paul's thought about salvation, and he draws on a number of contingent concepts to explain what salvation means and how it works.[1] In this chapter we shall explore the meaning and significance of some of these concepts.

Righteousness

One of Paul's most powerful images for salvation is that of 'righteousness', which is both the source and consequence of salvation. By that I mean that salvation begins because of the revelation of the 'righteousness of God', and the result is that believers are 'righteoused', or, in correct English, we say they are 'justified'. There are a lot of debates we could get into here but I shall refrain from engaging in them. Instead, I shall focus on the meaning of the 'righteousness of God' and 'justification' in Paul's theology of salvation.[2]

Paul mentions the 'righteousness of God' (*dikaiosynē theou*) several times (Rom. 1:17; 3:21–22; 10:3; 2 Cor. 5:21; and Phil. 3:9). Does it refer to (1) a *subjective* quality (God's own righteousness, like his moral uprightness, integrity or fidelity), or (2) an *objective* quality (the righteousness that comes from God)? In answer, several things must be considered.

First, we should locate this term in the context of *creation* and *covenant*. As Creator, God is determined to establish righteousness throughout all the earth (e.g. Gen. 18:25; 1 Chr. 16:33–34; Ps. 98:9). At the same time, God has covenanted with Israel: when he intervened to save Israel, he was acting in righteousness and

---

1. J. C. Beker, *Paul the Apostle: The Triumph of God in Life and Thought* (Philadelphia: Fortress, 1980), pp. 23–36; J. D. G. Dunn, *The Theology of Paul the Apostle* (Edinburgh: T. & T. Clark, 1998), p. 231.

2. For a global examination of the issues see M. F. Bird, *The Saving Righteousness of God: Studies in Paul, Justification, and the New Perspective*, PBM (Milton Keynes: Paternoster, 2007), pp. 6–39.

faithfulness to his covenant promises (e.g. Deut. 7:9; Pss 46:10–11; 111:7–8; Zech. 8:8). In saving Israel, God is faithful to his covenant and restores his people to covenant status.

Second, in the Old Testament and in Jewish literature more generally, 'righteousness' is often synonymous for 'salvation' (e.g. Judg. 5:11; 1 Sam. 12:7). In Isaiah we read, 'Maintain justice and do righteousness, for my salvation is about to come and my righteousness to be revealed' (Isa. 56:1).

Third, it seems better to understand 'righteousness of God' as a subjective genitive, that is, a righteousness that belongs to God, understood here as God's own saving activity. The reason is that the fullest exposition of the phrase as it appears in Romans stands in proximity and parallel to a whole host of other subjective genitives, including the 'power of God' (Rom. 1:16), the 'wrath of God' (Rom. 1:18; 3:5), the 'faithfulness of God' (Rom. 3:3) and the 'truthfulness of God' (Rom. 3:7; 15:8). These are all qualities or dispositions that belong to God himself. Thus, the righteousness of God is revealed in the gospel as the outworking of his own saving power.

Fourth, the 'righteousness of God' is manifested in Christ's sacrificial death and has the effect of restoring sinners to a right relationship with God (Rom. 3:21–25). There is also the gift of a righteous status (Rom. 5:15–19), and Paul once speaks of a righteousness that originates from God and becomes the possession of the believer (Phil. 3:9). But it is too much to say that 'righteousness of God' is merely a righteousness imputed from Jesus Christ and received by faith, as some interpreters are fond of taking it. The 'righteousness of God' is an all-encompassing act that implements the *entire plan of salvation*, including justification, redemption, atonement, forgiveness, membership in the new covenant community, reconciliation, the gift of the Holy Spirit, power for a new obedience, union with Christ, freedom from sin, and vindication at the final judgment. Arland Hultgren is right on the mark when he comments:

> When Paul speaks of the righteousness of God in this instance, and says that it is revealed in the gospel, he does not speak primarily of a righteousness that is imputed to believers. He is speaking of a righteousness revealed in the Gospel of God's Son, the saving message

of how God has sent his Son for the salvation of sinful humanity. God's righteousness is God's saving activity which is spoken of in the Scriptures of Israel and promised with the coming of the Messiah or the messianic age.[3]

We might therefore tabulate the various backgrounds and consequences of the 'righteousness of God' as it relates to Paul's gospel in the following way:

Spheres	Execution	Revelation in the Gospel
Creation	Punitive justice Restoration of creation Reaches the nations	Gift of a righteous status Life and resurrection Rectification of cosmos
Covenant	Faithfulness to the covenant Atonement for sin Deliverance of Israel	Redemption from sin Transformation to new life Membership in the new covenant

Paul often talks of 'justification', or the verbal form, being 'justified'. For example, 'For all have sinned and fall short of the glory of God; and they are now justified by his grace as a gift, through the redemption that is in Christ Jesus' (Rom. 3:23–24); and 'we have come to believe in Christ Jesus, so that we might be justified by faith in Christ, and not by works of the law' (Gal. 2:16). I have a four-pronged strategy for explaining what Paul means by 'justification'.

First, justification is *forensic*: it refers to a status one has before God. A person who is justified is declared right or acquitted of wrong. To be justified is the opposite of being condemned (Deut. 25:1; Rom. 8:1–3, 33–34; 2 Cor. 3:9). God does not justify the righteous, since no one is truly righteous before God based on their own merits (Rom. 3:20–23). God graciously justifies sinners, the wicked and the ungodly through the provision of setting forth

---

3. A. J. Hultgren, *Paul's Gospel and Mission* (Philadelphia: Fortress, 1983), p. 31.

Christ (Rom. 3:20–25; 4:5; 5:6). That is not because God pretends they are innocent, but because Jesus' death satisfies God's justice.

Second, justification is also *covenantal*. Paul's arguments about justification occur primarily in contexts where he defends the rights of Gentiles to be full members of the people of God as Gentiles without having to convert to Judaism in order to gain that status. Justification by faith implies fellowship by faith, as those who believe in Jesus are legitimated in their identity as members of the new-covenant community (Rom. 3:27 – 4:25; Gal. 2:11–21; 4:31; Eph. 2:11 – 3:6).

Third, justification is *eschatological*, as the verdict anticipated on the Day of Judgment in Jewish thinking has been declared in the present (Rom. 2:13–16; 8:31–34; Gal. 5:5). Indeed, the future verdicts are enacted in Jesus' death and resurrection, where God prosecutes his contention against people by handing over Jesus to atone for their sins, and enacts their justification by raising his Son from the dead (Rom. 4:25).

Fourth, justification is *effective* in that God's transforming power to free believers from the power of sin is the logical result of the declaration of acquittal (Rom. 6:7, 18). Thus, justification means that believers have been declared to be in a right relationship with God, a relationship initiated and sustained by God's saving righteousness. This verdict of acquittal means that believers have been delivered from the tripartite tyranny of law–sin–death, and equally shows that God has not limited his mercy and compassion to one ethnic race.

In sum, justification is the act whereby God creates a new people, with a new status, in a new covenant, as a foretaste of the new age.

But what about the imputation of Christ's righteousness as the basis of justification? That is the notion that God imputes the obedience and merits of Jesus to believers and in turn imputes their sins to Jesus on the cross. Well, the fact of the matter is that we cannot proof-text imputation. If we think we can cite 2 Corinthians 5:21, Romans 4:1–5, 1 Corinthians 1:30 or Philippians 3:6–9 and find the entire package of the imputation of Christ's active obedience and the imputation of our sin to Christ embedded in all of these texts, we are sadly mistaken. These texts all come close to saying something like that, but fall short of doing so. What is more, these passages are not replaying the same tune over and over, for each says something slightly different about Christ's work.[4]

At the level of the text, then, Paul argues that we are justified by union with Christ through what I have called 'incorporated righteousness'.[5] Jesus is justified in his resurrection, and by faith we have union with him so that we share in his justification. Through incorporation into Christ by faith, what is his becomes ours and what is ours becomes his. Now, before the doctrine police beat me to death with a copy of Calvin's *Institutes of the Christian Religion*, let me qualify what I have said so far.

The imputation of Christ's righteousness is a necessary and logical inference to make, as it allows us coherently to hold together a number of ideas and concepts in Paul's story of salvation. Although no text explicitly says that Christ's righteousness is imputed to believers, nonetheless, without some kind of theology of imputation a lot of what Paul says about justification does not make sense. Imputation is a synthetic way of holding together a number of themes that clearly point in the direction of imputation, or something very much akin to it. I have tried to show in the figure below how imputation is the integrating point for a variety of ideas in Paul's letters.

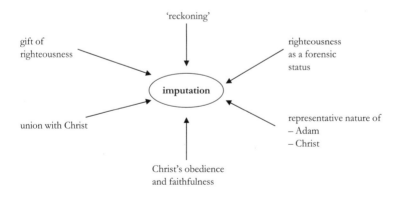

---

4. On which see the excellent study by B. Vickers, *Jesus' Blood and Righteousness: Paul's Theology of Imputation* (Wheaton: Crossway, 2006).

5. Bird, *Saving Righteousness of God*, pp. 60–87.

Taken together, the language of 'reckoning', the emphasis on Christ's obedience and faithfulness, the representative nature of Adam and Christ, the references to union with Christ, the fact that righteousness is explicitly called a 'gift' and the forensic nature of righteousness all make sense with some kind of theology of imputation. The mistake comes when scholars, even well-intentioned ones, try to read the entire package back into certain texts of Paul's letters – it just does not come out that way. I concur with Leon Morris, who said that imputation is a corollary of the identification of the believer with Christ.[6]

Sacrifice

'Sacrifice' means that Jesus pays the price for sin as a sacrifice of atonement. But even within this metaphor a variety of sub-metaphors are in operation.[7] The primary background for Paul's language of sacrifice and atonement is of course the Old Testament. Leviticus 1 – 7 gives instruction concerning the various sacrifices such as sin and grain offerings. There is the 'Day of Atonement', when the sins of Israel are transferred to a goat and the goat is driven out of the camp into the wilderness (Lev. 16:1–34; 23:26–32), and the rationale behind sacrificial offerings is that 'For the life of the animal is in the blood; and I have given it to you for making atonement for your lives on the altar; for it is the blood that makes atonement for one's life' (Lev. 17:11). The Suffering Servant of Isaiah 53 suffers vicariously for the nation of Israel: he is pierced for their transgressions, their guilt is laid upon him, he is made an offering for sin and justifies many by his sufferings.

---

6. L. Morris, *The Apostolic Preaching of the Cross*, 3rd ed. (Grand Rapids: Eerdmans, 1984), p. 282.

7. For the rich and multifaceted array of metaphors and meanings concerning the atonement see the classic work by J. Stott, *The Cross of Christ*, rev. ed. (Leicester: IVP, 1989); and more recently (and somewhat controversially), J. B. Green and M. D. Baker, *Recovering the Scandal of the Cross: Atonement in New Testament and Contemporary Contexts* (Carlisle, UK: Paternoster, 2000).

At this point it is illuminating to see how Jewish authors in the intertestamental period interpreted and applied this theology of sacrifice in their environment. In a Jewish document called 4 Maccabees, Eleazar pleads to God in view of his imminent martyrdom, 'Be merciful to your people, and let our punishment make recompense for them. Make my blood their purification, and take my life in exchange for theirs' (4 Macc. 6.28–29), which ascribed salvific value to his death.[8]

Nor was the idea of a sacrificial and salvific death unknown in Greco-Roman sources. Livy said that the Roman general Decius (c. 340 BC) died 'as though sent from heaven as an expiatory offering of all the anger of the gods, and to turn aside destruction from his people and bring it on their adversaries' (*AUC* 8.9.10). Plutarch wrote that the Spartan king Leonidas who died at the battle of Thermopylae was the one 'who, in obedience to the oracles, sacrifices himself, as it were then, for the sake [*hyper*] of Greece' (Plutarch, *Pel.* 20–21).

While some have tried to argue that Paul's idea of sacrifice and atonement is taken up from Hellenistic sources like the pagan mystery cults, this is far from certain, since a more immediate cache of sacrificial ideas was available to Paul through the Old Testament, and theological reflection about sacrifice was already extant in post-biblical Palestinian literature too (1 Macc. 6.44; 2 Macc. 7.37–38; 11QTgJob 38.2–3; 1QS 8.3–4; Prayer of Azariah 3.38–40; *LAB* 18.5; *T. Mos.* 9.6–10.1; *T. Benj.* 3.8; *LAE* 3.1).

About Paul's theology of 'sacrifice' we can note, first, that Paul frequently applies the language of sacrifice and cultic imagery to Jesus' death (Rom. 3:25; 8:3; 1 Cor. 5:7; 2 Cor. 5:21). The meaning of the words for sacrifice (*thyō* and *thysia*) is 'that which is killed or offered in sacrifice'.[9] It is Jesus' death as a sacrifice that lies behind Paul's remark that 'For what the law was powerless to do in that it was weakened by the flesh, God did by sending his own Son in the

---

8. On the relation of 4 Maccabees 6.28–29 to Isa. 53 see D. A. deSilva,
   4 Maccabees: Introduction and Commentary on the Greek Text of Codex Sinaiticus,
   SCS (Leiden: Brill, 2006), pp. 147–148.

9. BDAG, pp. 462–463.

likeness of sinful flesh to be a sin offering. And so he condemned
sin in the flesh' (Rom. 8:3). N. T. Wright comments:

> No clearer statement is found in Paul, or indeed anywhere else in all early
> Christian literature, of the early Christian belief that what happened on
> the cross was the judicial punishment of sin. Taken in conjunction with
> 8:1 and the whole argument of the passage, not to mention the partial
> parallels in 2 Cor 5:21 and Gal 3:13, it is clear that Paul intends to say that
> in Jesus' death the damnation that sin deserved was meted out fully and
> finally, so that sinners over whose heads that condemnation had hung
> might be liberated from this threat once and for all.[10]

Second, the death of Jesus is sometimes presented in a way reminiscent of the Aqedah, Abraham's willingness to offer up Isaac. A
comparison of Romans 8:32 ('he did not spare his own son') and
Genesis 22:16 ('you did not spare your own/beloved son') makes the
similarities obvious. The connection is that God offered his Son in
much the same way Abraham offered Isaac, namely to be a sacrifice.
In the case of Romans 8:1–3 and Galatians 4:4–5, the purpose of
the 'sending' of the Son is for him to be a sin-offering and to redeem
those under the curse of the law. In Jewish literature of the time,
there is a tendency to interpret the Aqedah in vicarious terms (e.g.
Philo, *Abr.* 172), and Paul may witness to that trend as well when he
echoes the idea in relation to Jesus' death.

Third, another image is that of Christ as a Passover lamb: 'For
our paschal lamb, Christ, has been sacrificed' (1 Cor. 5:7). Christ's
death is the precursor to a new exodus: he dies for a purpose iden-
tical to that of the lambs slaughtered in place of the firstborn
from each Hebrew family.[11] This is a good example of

---

10. N. T. Wright, 'Romans', in *New Interpreters Bible*, ed. L. E. Keck, 12 vols.
    (Abingdon: Nashville, 2002), vol. 10, pp. 574–575.
11. Passover and atonement for sins are specifically linked in Ezek.
    45:18–22 and at Jesus' interpretation of his own death at the last supper
    (Mark 14:24). On the significance of Passover imagery in Paul see
    T. Holland, *Contours of Pauline Theology* (Fearn, Ross-shire: Christian
    Focus, 2004).

substitution, where the lamb died in the place of, or instead of, the firstborn of each family.[12]

Fourth, Paul also says about Jesus' death that 'God set [him] forth as a *hilastērion*, through faith in his blood' (Rom. 3:25). The debate is whether the word *hilastērion* designates (1) the *place* of atonement being the 'mercy seat' of Leviticus 16 (Tyndale, NET), (2) the *means* of atonement being either 'expiation' as the removal and cancellation of sin (NAB, RSV), or (3) 'propitiation' as the appeasement of God's wrath (NKJV, ESV, NASB).[13] The only other occurrence of this word in the New Testament is in Hebrews 9:5, where it refers to the mercy seat (the same is true of occurrences of the word in the Septuagint). The problem, though, is how the sacrifice sprinkled on the mercy seat impacts sin and God's attitude towards it. During the mid-twentieth century there was a debate between C. H. Dodd (who argued for expiation) and Leon Morris (who argued for propitiation). I confess that I am persuaded by the arguments of Morris that propitiation is the correct meaning here.

What is more, the propitiation interpretation makes good sense of the broader context of Romans. Earlier, Paul refers to the revelation of the 'wrath of God' against all wickedness and ungodliness (Rom. 1:18), which stands in juxtaposition to the manifestation of the 'righteousness of God' that provides atonement and redemption for the sin that invoked God's wrath (Rom. 3:21–26). But we do not have to insist on false bifurcations, since Jesus is both the *place* of atonement (lit. meaning of *hilastērion*) and the *means* of atonement (broader context of Romans 1 – 8). God's wrath is exercised against sin; thus, when sin is expiated, God is propitiated. Now if God is the one who set Jesus forth as a sacrifice of propitiation and if God is the one propitiated, then it means that God is in effect propitiating himself. While some might say this is an incoherent line of thought, I suggest that it is the glorious mystery of the cross: the initiative and provision for

---

12. M. D. Hooker, *Jesus and the Servant* (London: SPCK, 1959), p. 77.

13. The NIV and NRSV try to have a bet both ways by offering a translation of 'sacrifice of atonement'.

the atonement of sin comes from the very God offended by that sin.[14]

A common way to express what we find in these texts is the label 'penal substitution'.[15] We can define this as the view that God punishes Jesus for our sins by putting him in our place on the cross. The 'penal' nature of Christ's death is established (1) by Romans 8:3, which states that God 'condemned sin in the flesh' of his Son, and (2) the reference to propitiation concerning the appeasement of wrath in Romans 3:25. The element of 'substitution' in Christ's death is also implied in several other texts, such as 1 Corinthians 5:7, Galatians 3:13 and 1 Timothy 2:6, and from the fact that Christ died 'for our sins', which carries the connotation that he died in our place. Jesus' death has an *exclusive* sense in that he takes the place of sinners, even though he himself is not a sinner.

We must also be careful not to read the entire package of penal substitution into every text about Jesus' death. For example, Paul says, 'For our sake he [God] made him to be sin who knew no sin, so that in him we might become the righteousness of God' (2 Cor. 5:21). What is going on here might be expressed better as 'interchange' or 'transference' rather than 'substitution'.[16] There is a reversal so that the one who knew no sin becomes sin and bears

---

14. See D. A. Carson, 'Atonement in Romans 3:21–26', in *The Glory of the Atonement: Biblical, Theological, and Practical Perspectives*, ed. C. E. Hill and F. A. James (Downers Grove: IVP; Leicester: Apollos, 2004), pp. 130–135.

15. For a recent defence of penal substitution see S. Jeffery, M. Ovey and A. Sach, *Pierced for our Transgressions: Rediscovering the Glory of Penal Substitution* (Nottingham: IVP, 2007); T. R. Schreiner, 'Penal Substitution View', in *The Nature of the Atonement: Four Views*, ed. P. R. Eddy and J. K. Beilby (Downers Grove: IVP, 2006), pp. 67–98; S. Holmes, 'Can Punishment Bring Peace? Penal Substitution Revisited', *SJT* 58 (2005), pp. 104–123; A. T. B. McGowan, 'The Atonement as Penal Substitution', in *Always Reforming: Explorations in Systematic Theology*, ed. A. T. B. McGowan (Leicester: Apollos, 2006), pp. 183–210; and the classic essay by J. I. Packer, 'What Did the Cross Achieve? The Logic of Penal Substitution', *TynBul* 25 (1974), pp. 3–45.

16. M. D. Hooker, 'Interchange in Christ', *JTS* 22 (1971), p. 353; R. P. Martin, *2 Corinthians*, WBC (Waco: Word, 1986), p. 144.

the sin and its penalty, while those genuinely guilty of sin become innocent, pure and acquitted through the transaction of sacrifice. That interchange or transference happens in the humanity of Christ, who through his obedience is able to undo the sin and condemnation of Adam in the cross.

On another level, we have to affirm that Jesus is also the representative of believers. While there is a portrayal of Jesus as suffering judgment in our place, in a sense we do not get away scot-free. Believers are saved only because they participate in Christ's death. Paul makes this point a number of times: 'I have been crucified with Christ and I no longer live' (Gal. 2:20) and 'For we know that our old self was crucified with him so that the body of sin might be done away with' (Rom. 6:6). God exercises his judgment and pours out his wrath on Christ, and because Christ is the representative of believers it means they have entered into that experience of judgment and wrath as well. The logic is that because they have gone through it once they can never go through it again. What is more, in the same way that they share in Christ's death and the associated judgment, they also share in his resurrection and associated vindication (Rom. 6:4–5; Col. 2:12; 3:1; Eph. 2:6).

This helps us to make sense of two disputed texts in Paul. Paul states in Romans, 'just as the result of one trespass was condemnation for all men, so also the result of one act of righteousness was justification that brings life for *all men*' (Rom. 5:18), and 2 Corinthians, 'For Christ's love compels us, because we are convinced that one died for all, and therefore *all* died' (2 Cor. 5:14). These passages are not teaching a kind of quasi-universalism that the death of Christ guarantees the salvation of all human beings. While it may be possible to correlate the 'all/all men' with 'all believers', we should take seriously the representative function of Jesus as the second Adam who represents humanity. Jesus is the representative of the whole human race and his death signifies that all human beings must undergo death. They can either enter death in the second Adam, who experiences death for them, or else can undergo death themselves.

Paul's point is that the death of Jesus is the singular determining factor for the destiny of the entire human race in relation to God. The death of Jesus Christ is the only way in which human beings can experience death, judgment and wrath and yet live. Death and judgment are inescapable, but by virtue of participating in and identifying with Christ's death, neither sin nor death nor wrath have the last word.[17] In this sense, Jesus' death is *inclusive*, as Jesus is a member of humanity and suffers for humanity. Jesus then stands as the representative of the human race: all humans can experience judgment *in him* through the judgment executed *upon him*. Since the representative is also the substitute, any person (if he or she repents) can emerge through the ordeal of judgment and death with life and acquittal. Thus, substitution presupposes representation, and only because Jesus is our representative can he also be our substitute.

To put it in other words, it is only because Jesus shares our humanity (inclusiveness) that he as the sinless one can bear our sin in our place (exclusiveness). Although F. C. Baur does not adequately distinguish substitution from representation, he accurately captures the logic of Paul's thinking:

> The idea of substitution implies two things, first, that the one who is to take the place of many others, and to be counted for them, is the same as they are; and secondly, that he possesses something which they have not; that, namely the lack of which makes it necessary that he should represent them. If Christ has died for the sins of men, then he must have been without sin himself, in order that his death, which could not be a sacrifice on his own account, might avail as the penalty of the sins of others.[18]

Reconciliation

Another image is that of 'reconciliation', which is taken from the world of relationships. It refers to the restoration of relationships between persons such as husband and wife (1 Cor. 7:11) and between fellow Israelites (Acts 7:26). Paul speaks of humanity

---

17. Dunn, *Theology of Paul the Apostle*, pp. 210–211, 223.
18. F. C. Baur, *Paul the Apostle of Jesus Christ: His Life and Works, His Epistles and Teachings: Two Volumes in One* (Peabody: Hendrickson, 2003 [1873–5]), vol. 2, pp. 155–156.

being reconciled to God (Rom. 5:10–11; 2 Cor. 5:18–21; Eph. 2:14–17; Col. 1:20–22). The key word here is *katalassō*, which basically means, 'The exchange of hostility for a friendly relationship.'[19]

Several Jewish authors also speak of reconciliation. For example, Josephus describes Moses in his role as a mediator between God and the people: 'When Moses had spoken to them, according to the decision of God, the multitude became grieved in their affliction, and pleaded with Moses to procure their reconciliation to God, and to permit them to no longer wander in the wilderness' (*Ant.* 3.315). Josephus also gives an account of how a cohort of Roman infantry were foolishly ambushed during the siege of Jerusalem. Titus angrily sought to inflict severe discipline upon them because of their foolishness, but at the petition of his commanders relented. Josephus writes, 'he was reconciled to the soldiers, but gave them special orders to act more wisely in the future; and he considered with himself how he might get even with the Jews for their stratagem' (*War* 5.129). In 2 Maccabees, one of the martyrs states, 'And if our living Lord is angry for a little while, to rebuke and discipline us, he will again be reconciled with his own servants' (2 Macc. 7.33). This is the background to what Paul says, especially in Romans 5:1–11 and 2 Corinthians 5:14–21.

What is significant, though, as Stanley Porter has argued, is that Paul was the first author to speak of the offended party (God) initiating reconciliation, and using the verb *katallassō* (I reconcile) in the active voice.[20] According to Paul, reconciliation starts with God, who reaches out in grace. It does not begin with the offending party reaching out for peace and forgiveness. In this sense, reconciliation is an expression of God's grace. For this reason, some scholars have argued, with good reason too, that reconciliation is the central theme of Paul's theology of salvation.[21]

In 2 Corinthians, Paul writes, 'All this is from God, who through

---

19. BDAG, p. 521.

20. S. E. Porter, Katalassō *in Ancient Greek Literature, with Reference to the Pauline Writings* (Cordoba: Ediciónes El Almendro, 1994).

21. R. P. Martin, *Reconciliation: A Study of Paul's Theology* (Atlanta: Westminster John Knox, 1981); Marshall, *New Testament Theology*, pp. 719–720.

Christ reconciled us to himself and gave us the ministry of reconciliation; that is, God was in Christ reconciling the world to himself,
not counting their trespasses against them, and entrusting to us the
message of reconciliation' (2 Cor. 5:18–19). And in Romans, he
states, 'For if while we were enemies we were reconciled to God by
the death of his Son, how much more then, having been reconciled, shall we be saved through his life. Moreover, we boast in God
through our Lord Jesus Christ, through whom we have now
received reconciliation' (Rom. 5:10–11).

Reconciliation has a global and cosmic scope, as the world alienated from God is brought back to God. This reconciliation is
available exclusively through the cross. In Colossians, Paul wonderfully blends the cosmic result and crucicentric mechanism for
reconciliation: '[God was pleased] through him to reconcile to
himself all things, whether on earth or in heaven, making peace by
the blood of his cross. And you, who once were alienated and
hostile in thought, doing evil deeds, he has now reconciled in his
body of flesh by his death' (Col. 1:20–22).

What accompanies reconciliation is the unity of Jews and Gentiles
in one body, since the dividing wall between them has been broken
down and they are united so that God 'might reconcile us both to God
in one body through the cross, thereby killing the hostility' (Eph. 2:16).
Reconciliation emerges as a counterpart to justification. It marks the
end of alienation and hostilities between humanity and God, it mends
the rupture in the Creator–creature relationship, it occurs through or
in Christ (specifically his death), God no longer reckons sin to sinners
and it results in peace – not peace as a subjective experience, but the
objective state of peace between warring parties.

Redemption

Salvation as 'redemption' is another metaphor at Paul's disposal, and
he employs it at several points (Rom. 3:24; 8:23; 1 Cor. 1:30;
6:19–20; Gal. 3:13; 4:5; Col. 1:14; Eph. 1:7, 14; 4:30; 1 Tim. 2:6; Tit.
2:14). Like much of Paul's thought, this image has both a Jewish and
Greco-Roman background. In the Old Testament, the great act of
redemption was the exodus from Egypt (e.g. Exod. 6:6; Deut. 7:8;

9:26; 13:5; 15:15; 24:18; 1 Chr. 17:21; Neh. 1:10; Pss 77:15; 78:42; Mic. 6:4). It was the epochal moment where God remembered his promises to the patriarchs and redeemed his people from slavery. This was thereafter celebrated at every Passover. What is more, just as God once redeemed Israel from slavery and bondage, so too the prophets announced that God would *again* redeem Israel in a new exodus from exile (e.g. Isa. 43:1–7; 48:20; 51:10–11; 62:12; Jer. 16:14–15; 31:11–12; Mic. 4:10; Zech. 10:8).

In the Old Testament are places where individuals thank God for redeeming them from sin (Pss 19:14; 103:3–4; 130:8) and death (Job. 33:28; Pss 49:15; 103:3–4; Hos. 13:14). Whereas the first exodus from Egypt was celebrated by the Passover, for Paul Jesus' death achieved a *new exodus* celebrated in the Lord's Supper as the memorial meal for God's greatest deliverance: freeing captives from the bonds of sin and death. Redemption was also an integral part of the covenantal regulations concerning debts and justice. Leviticus 25 has instructions pertaining to 'kinsman redeemers' who are relatives, who can redeem property sold because of debt and redeem persons sold into slavery (Lev. 25:25, 47–55).

In Exodus 21, we find a redemption scheme pertaining to accidental death and personal injuries. If a bull habitually gores people, if the owner fails to keep the bull penned and if the bull subsequently kills someone, then 'the owner must be put to death'. A reprieve can be granted if payment is made, and then the owner 'may redeem his life by paying whatever is demanded' (Exod. 21:28–32).

This is analogous to the Greco-Roman context of redemption that has to do with the manumission of slaves and repatriation of prisoners of war when the appropriate price is paid. This underscores that redemption meant freedom from slavery and salvation from death.[22] Which is why Paul says that believers participate in Christ's death: so they will no longer be 'slaves of sin' (Rom. 6:6). Elsewhere he writes, 'You were bought at a price; do not become

---

22. In the case of 'sacral manumission', slaves were fictitiously purchased by a local deity who subsequently freed them. The owner accompanied the slave to the temple, sold him or her to the god and received the money from the temple treasury (the slave having previously paid the price out of

slaves of men' (1 Cor. 7:23), and entering the life of the age to come is called the final act of 'redemption' (Rom. 8:23; Eph. 1:14; 4:30).

Redemption has various associations for Paul. It is related to the forgiveness of sins (Col. 1:14; Eph. 1:7), righteousness and holiness (1 Cor. 1:30); it occurs through Christ's 'sacrifice' or 'blood' (Rom. 3:24–25; Eph. 1:7); Christ saves believers from the curses associated with the law-covenant (Gal. 3:13; 4:5), and from wickedness (Tit. 2:14). Paul can even say that Jesus is a 'ransom' for all men (1 Tim. 2:6; cf. Mark 10:45/Matt. 20:28). While it is tempting to say that in redemption Christ pays our *price* rather than takes our *place*, nonetheless, in Galatians 3:13 Paul states that Christ redeemed us from the curse of the law by becoming 'a curse for us', or by enduring the curse in our stead. This implies that redemption occurs through substitution.

We must also add a much neglected aspect, that believers are saved for the purpose of living a godly life and showing forth righteous behaviour. Christ redeems people so that they are no longer 'slaves to sin' (Rom. 6:6), also 'to purify for himself a people that are his very own, eager to do what is good' (Tit. 2:14), and finally Paul admonishes the Corinthians that 'You are not your own, you were bought at a price, therefore, honour God with your body' (1 Cor. 6:19b–20; cf. Gal. 5:1, 13). According to Paul, redemption means becoming Christ's slave and being dedicated to the purposes and pattern of life summed up in Christ.

Adoption

Another metaphor used by Paul to describe salvation is that of 'adoption', or how Christians attain sonship in God's family. In

---

Footnote 22 (*continued*)

his or her own funds). One ancient inscription reads, 'Apollo the Pythian bought from Sisibius of Amphissa, for freedom, a female slave, whose name is Nicea, by race a Roman, with a price of three minae of silver and a half-mina. Former seller according to the law: Eumnastus of Amphissa. The price he hath received. The purchase, however, Nicea has committed unto Apollo for freedom' (*LANE*, pp. 322–323).

THE *CRUX* OF THE GOSPEL

Roman law, *adoptio* was the process whereby an adoptee shifted from being under the authority of his own family head (*paterfamilias*) to being under the authority of his adopted father. The adoptee would then become a member of the new household and sometimes even be the sole heir to the father's estate. For Paul, adoption or acquiring sonship meant becoming part of God's people. While the word for adoption (*huiothesia*) does not occur in the Greek version of the Old Testament, the idea of Israel as 'sons' of God is present (e.g. Exod. 4:22; Hos. 11:1).

In Galatians, Paul writes that God sent his son to redeem those under the law so that 'we might receive adoption as sons' (Gal. 4:5), and in Romans he states, 'you have received the Spirit of adoption as sons' (Rom. 8:15). Because believers are sons, they are no longer slaves and have been given the Spirit of God, through whom they are able to cry out, 'Abba, Father!' (Gal. 4:6–7; Rom. 8:15–16). They are now part of Abraham's family, which is also Christ's family, and are consequently heirs of God's promises and even co-heirs with Christ (Gal. 3:29; Rom. 8:17). The transfer is a radical one, since believers have shifted from being heirless and fatherless slaves to being co-heirs with Christ, fathered by the Creator God.

Two further points are noteworthy. First, Paul links adoption closely with redemption (Gal. 4:4–5; Rom. 8:23). While redemption and adoption are a present experience, they are also something to be awaited more fully in the future. As Christians wait for the 'redemption' of their bodies, they also 'wait eagerly for adoption as sons', which gives a wide eschatological span to the act of being and becoming sons of God. Second, adoption occurs in the messianic Son of God, and Jesus is the broker or means through which the former slaves of sin and death are brought into the family of God and are granted the promises and blessings that go with being in Christ Jesus.[23]

---

23. On adoption in the New Testament see the fine study by T. J. Burke, *Adopted into God's Family: Exploring a Pauline Metaphor*, NSBT 22 (Nottingham: Apollos; Downers Grove: IVP, 2006).

Renewal

Salvation is not in Paul's view a one-time accomplishment that God did on the cross. Salvation is as much about God's work in the present life of the believer as it is about God's work in the past and future. God is continually working his saving power into the lives of believers. In a call to obedience, Paul writes to the Philippians, 'work out your salvation with fear and trembling, for it is God who works in you to will and to act according to his good purpose' (Phil. 2:12–13). Believers are to work out what God has worked in. We might call this God's work of renewal, an idea that often appears through Paul's use of the words *anakainoō* (I renew) and *anakainōsis* (renewal).

In 2 Corinthians, Paul can list the harrowing trials and afflictions he encountered, even being given over to death. He takes solace from the fact that 'Even though our outer nature is wasting away, our inner nature is being renewed day by day' (2 Cor. 4:16). The degenerative effect that trials have upon the Christian cannot overcome the regenerative power of God in sustaining them. Christian ministers should take comfort from the fact that if God intends to *use them*, then in the course of time he *renews them* in order to continue the work to which he has called them.

In the opening exhortation of Romans 12, Paul urges the Romans, 'Do not be conformed to this age, but be transformed by the renewing of your mind' (Rom. 12:2). Christians are to go against the grain of this world by making sure that the things they esteem and value line up with what God esteems and values. Only a renewed mind can think the things of God. Similarly, Paul can command believers 'to be renewed in the spirit of your minds and to clothe yourselves with the new man, created according to the likeness of God in righteousness and holiness' (Eph. 4:23–24). That forms the reverse side of his command to put off the old way of life and to put away sinful behaviours.

By analogy, we might say that Paul is telling the Ephesians that they are somewhat like a computer suite that has been upgraded with brand-new state-of-the-art hardware. Therefore, stop trying to load old virus-ridden software onto this pristine new hardware. The well-known text Titus 3:5–6 says, 'he saved us not by works of righteousness which we have done but according to his mercy, through the washing of rebirth and by renewal of the Holy Spirit, whom he poured out on us richly through Jesus Christ our Saviour'. The obvious point here is that new birth or being 'born again' is accompanied by the renewing work of the Holy Spirit at the beginning of the Christian life.

I am not a big fan of bumper-sticker theology: that is, sticking pithy theological slogans onto the bumper of a car. I particularly dislike the one 'Christians are not perfect, just forgiven'. While true at one level, it overlooks the crucial ingredient in the Christian life being the renewing power of God working in us through the Spirit. It might be better to write, 'Christians are not perfect, but God is at work in them through the vitalizing power of the Holy Spirit to transform these cracked jars of clay into glorious vessels of holiness, righteousness and good-ness' – if only bumper stickers were that big! In Paul's writings, renewal is the process of transformation into the image of God that is realized through the operation of God's glory and via the agency of the Spirit. The Spirit is continually at work in believers to make them less like themselves and more like God's Son.

Victory

Finally, according to Paul, Jesus' death is a victory over sin, death and the spiritual powers of the evil age. In the first thousand years of Christianity, the most frequent way of explaining what the cross achieved was through what is called the 'ransom theory' of the atonement. That is the view that God handed over Jesus to the devil as a ransom for believers. The devil foolishly thought he could hold Jesus in the bonds of death and hell when in fact he could not, and Jesus rose from the grave in victory over the devil. Thus the devil was duped, since he took the bait (Christ's flesh) and got caught on the hook (Christ's divinity). While we may remain uncomfortable with certain parts of that analogy, there is one part we should maintain, namely that Jesus' death and resurrection are a cosmic victory over the dark forces of this evil age.[24]

In a remarkable text from Colossians, Paul can say that God, having 'disarmed the rulers and authorities, he has made a public debacle of them, triumphing over them by the cross' (Col. 2:15). What appeared to the spiritual rulers and principalities as God's apparent defeat on the cross was in fact the occasion for his greatest triumph. John Chrysostom commented on this passage:

> Never yet was the devil in so shameful a plight. For while expecting to have him, he lost even those he had, and when Christ's body was nailed to the cross, the dead arose. At the cross death received his wound, having met his death stroke from a dead body. And as an athlete, when he thinks he has hit his adversary, himself is caught in a fatal grasp, so truly does Christ also show, that to die with arrogance is the devil's shame.[25]

The theme of God's defeat of Satan is made explicit at the end of Romans: 'The God of peace will soon crush Satan under your feet' (Rom. 16:20).

In the Roman world, a *triumphus* was a parade where a conquering general or king returned to Rome amid accolades and acclaim from the crowd. During the procession for his victory, he travelled along the main thoroughfare of the city (the Via Sacra) on a chariot pulled by four horses, with his troops behind him, booty and captives preceding him, and he ascended the Capitol to offer sacrifices in the temple of Jupiter. Paul can employ his image negatively where he likens himself and his fellow workers to the prisoners of war waiting to be executed at the end of the triumphal procession (1 Cor. 4:9). Elsewhere he depicts Christ as the *triumphator*, or conquering general, whose triumph he shares. He

24. The classic work on this subject remains G. Aulén, *Christus Victor: An Historical Study of the Three Main Types of the Idea of Atonement*, trans. A. G. Herber (New York: Macmillan, 1977).

25. Cited from P. Gorday (ed.), *Colossians, 1–2 Thessalonians, 1–2 Timothy, Titus, Philemon*, ACCS 9 (Downers Grove: IVP, 2000), p. 35.

writes, 'But thanks be to God, who always leads us in triumphal procession in Christ and through us spreads everywhere the fragrance of the knowledge of him' (2 Cor. 2:14). And in Ephesians, the ascension of Jesus is treated like a royal triumph, where, 'When he ascended on high he led a host of captives, and he gave gifts to men' (Eph. 4:8/Ps. 68:18); and the gifts the ascended Jesus gives his church are the offices of apostle, prophet, evangelist and teaching-shepherd.

Death can be treated as a personified personal enemy of God's people, which is why Paul can write, 'the last enemy to be destroyed is death' (1 Cor. 15:26). Death and its allies of sin and law meet their conqueror in the crucified and risen Christ. As such, 'The sting of death is sin, and the power of sin is the law. But thanks be to God, who gives us the victory through our Lord Jesus Christ' (1 Cor. 15:56–57). I am usually critical of preachers who engage in Greek word-studies in sermons, but one word that deserves a sermon on its own is *hyperkrinōmen*, 'we are hyper-conquerors', from Romans 8:37–39:

> [I]n all these things we are *hyper-conquerors* through him who loved us. For I am convinced that neither death, nor life, nor angels, nor rulers, nor things present, nor things to come, nor powers, nor height, nor depth, nor anything else in all creation will be able to separate us from the love of God in Christ Jesus our Lord.

The proclamation of the cross sounds like folly to many, when in fact it is God's wisdom: what looks like powerlessness is God's power; what sounds like a tragedy is a stunning victory; the death that looks so shameful has established God's honour; and what appears as a cause to mourn is a cause for inexpressible joy. God has triumphed in the cross of Jesus, and we share the triumph with him.

7. THE RETURN OF THE KING

The end of ages in Christ: Paul's eschatology

As an undergraduate student I had to read through G. E. Ladd's *A Theology of the New Testament* (a superb volume),[1] and I remember thinking that the word 'eschatology' must occur on nearly every page of the book. That left me pondering whether New Testament theology is really an expression of New Testament eschatology. Ten years of study later I am convinced that this is indeed the case. Eschatology is the study of the last things or the age to come. Fundamental to Paul's theology is that the future age (the eschaton) has already broken in and has been *inaugurated* through the life, death and resurrection of the Son of God.

At the same time, believers still await the final fulfilment or consummation of God's saving purposes at the parousia, or return of Jesus Christ, where the messianic kingdom begins and death is finally defeated. We are between two worlds, one beginning and

---

1. Rev. ed., ed. D. A. Hagner (Grand Rapids: Eerdmans, 1993).

one gradually fading away. It means that believers live in the time of the already and the not-yet, somewhat like living between the D-Day and VE Day of World War Two.[2] This framework is definitive for Paul's thinking and defines his world view and where he saw himself in the cosmic calendar. It was this conviction that also set him apart from many of his fellow Jews. Albert Schweitzer said:

> While other believers held that the finger of the world-clock was touching on the beginning of the coming hour and were waiting for the stroke which should announce this, Paul told them that it had already passed beyond the point, and that they had failed to hear the striking of the hour, which in fact struck at the Resurrection of Jesus.[3]

Saul the Pharisee believed that there were two ages: the present evil age and the age to come. He was living in the present evil age and waiting for the age to come and the advent of God's kingdom and the Messiah. On the Damascus road that hope was shattered when Saul realized that the age to come had already embryonically arrived in the resurrection of Jesus. According to Paul, Jesus Christ is the one through whom 'the end of ages has come' (1 Cor. 10:11), as his resurrection and the giving of the Spirit mark the partial arrival of the future age in the here and now. The two ages now overlap. The resurrection of Christ is the first fruits of the future age (1 Cor. 15:20, 23) and he is the firstborn of the general resurrection (Rom. 8:29; Col. 1:15, 18).

Similarly, the gift of the Spirit is the deposit of the new age yet to come in its fullness (2 Cor. 1:22; 5:5; Eph. 1:13–14) and it is given to strengthen believers until the parousia of the Lord (1 Cor. 1:7). This tension of the 'now' and the 'not-yet' influences Paul's understanding of salvation, which is why 'redemption', 'freedom', 'inheritance' and 'righteousness' can be spoken of as something

---

2. O. Cullmann, *Christ and Time*, trans. F. V. Filson (Philadelphia: Westminster, 1950), p. 84.

3. A. Schweitzer, *Mysticism of Paul the Apostle*, trans. W. Montgomery (Baltimore: Johns Hopkins University Press, 1998 [1931]), p. 99.

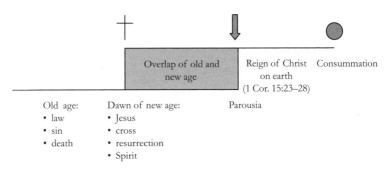

Pauline eschatology

believers participate in during the present time but also as something they anticipate for the future. We can pictorialize Paul's
eschatology as in the figure above.

The coming of Jesus has inaugurated a new era of redemptive
history and God's new age has been launched upon the world,
something like a covert operation seizing key nodes along the rear
echelons of an opposing force. Those people who confess faith in
the Messiah and experience the transforming power of the Spirit
of God are living billboards in our global metropolis advertising
God's activity in the world and pointing to things soon to come. At
the same time, the old age continues, death and evil are realities
that need to be confronted and endured, but their power has been
broken in principle and even in practice. What is more, the day is
coming when God will finally do away with them and the old age
will be no more. On that day God will be 'all in all' (1 Cor. 15:28).

Trying to understand Paul's eschatology can be a bit mind-
boggling at times, even more so if you try to correlate it with
events, language and descriptions from the book of Revelation. It
is tempting for us to resort to being 'pan-millennial', the belief that
it will all pan out at the end. Then again, we should not ignore the
seriousness of Paul's eschatological teaching, which involves
defending the gospel (1 Cor. 15) and providing hope to those in
distress (1 Thess. 4). While Paul does not want believers to become
'eschatomaniacs', end-times fruitcakes or a doomsday cult, he still
urges them 'not to be uninformed' of the doctrine of the last
things (1 Thess. 4:13). So, I suggest, get excited about Paul's

eschatology, take it seriously, but avoid becoming fixated on dates and timetables.

Before the end: the lawless one and the fate of Israel

Paul is intimately aware that before Christ comes there will be a time of suffering, temptation and tribulation. He experiences that in his own ministry (see esp. 1 Cor. 4:9–13; 2 Cor. 1:8–11; 12:1–10) and can even say that in his own perils 'he fills up the things lacking in the afflictions of Christ in my flesh on behalf of his body, the church' (Col. 1:24). What lies behind this verse is the belief that the arrival of the new age will be preceded by a time of suffering often called the 'birth pangs' (cf. Mark 13:8; Matt. 24:8; 1 Thess. 5:3). Christ's death was vicarious, protective and saved his flock from perishing in the messianic woes and the 'wrath' of the final judgment (Rom. 5:9; 1 Thess. 1:10; 5:9),[4] but, at the same time, believers can share in Jesus' sufferings as they live between the ages (Rom. 8:17–18; 2 Cor. 1:5–6; Phil. 1:29; 3:10; 1 Thess. 3:4). Paul describes himself as following Christ's example and vicariously suffering this affliction on behalf of others. That might mean that the persecutions and imprisonments suffered by Paul draw the attention of authorities away from his converts, who might otherwise experience similar afflictions if it were not for his drawing attention to himself.

In the Thessalonian correspondence, more instruction on this subject is given. In 1 Thessalonians 4–5, Paul assures his audience that those who die before the parousia will not miss out on the day of resurrection. When Paul says that God did not appoint believers to suffer wrath, he means the wrath of the final judgment, not the wrath of a final tribulation (1 Thess. 5:9). The suffering of the final ordeal will include persecutions and it would be odd for Paul to say that God intends the Thessalonians to avoid such persecutions,

---

4. See S. McKnight, *Jesus and His Death: Historiography, the Historical Jesus, and Atonement Theory* (Waco: Baylor University Press, 2005), for further argument on this point.

when in 1 Thessalonians 1–2 Paul commends them precisely for their endurance under suffering and persecution. The natural reading of 2 Thessalonians 2:1–12 is that the coming of the Lord is preceded by the coming of the lawless one who is destroyed at the advent of Christ.

On a point of application, those of us in the Western world should keep the persecuted church uppermost in our prayers. The saints in North Africa, the Middle East, China, North Korea, Turkey and South Asia fill up in their flesh the afflictions that are also ours. Perhaps the day will come when secular fundamentalism (for not all fundamentalisms are religious) will facilitate lawsuits, imprisonments and persecutions against Christians in the West if they fail to worship at the pantheon of religious pluralism and pansexuality.[5] Should that day come, we should not only pray, 'Lord deliver us from evil,' but, as a missionary friend once told me about the prayers of Christians in Asia, we should also pray, 'Lord give me a strong back in the face of suffering.' Our churches, some American ones in particular, need to spend less time telling non-Christians how to cope with being 'left behind' and start teaching Christians that to know Christ means to have fellowship with his sufferings and to be conformed to his death (Phil. 3:10)! For one day the prosperity bubble will burst and the lawless one will be revealed.

Paul also holds out hope that, before the end, Israel will be driven to jealousy and the Jewish nation, in whole or in part, will turn to Christ in faith. In Romans, Paul is doing some preventative pastoral care to stop the churches in Rome splitting along ethnic lines or dividing into factions based on various levels of adherence to the Jewish law. In particular, Paul wants to make sure that the Gentile Christians in Rome do not imitate the anti-Judaism of the cultural elites in Rome (read Tacitus, *Hist.* 5.5, to see what Romans thought about Jews). Paul argues that the gospel is first for the Jew, then the Gentile, not the Gentile instead of the Jew, as if God has written off Israel.

---

5. Christians in Canada who profess an orthodox faith might say that the day is coming and now is.

In Romans 11, the apostle argues that God has not completely rejected Israel (Rom. 11:1–2). Indeed, God has already called a remnant of Jewish Christians who believe in Jesus, and they are further proof that God's call and election of the nation remains irrevocable (Rom. 11:3–6). The failure of national Israel to believe in the Messiah has given occasion for the gospel to reach the Gentiles. This will, he hopes, provoke the nation to jealousy so that they might finally respond in faith. Paul argues from the lesser to the greater when he suggests that if Israel's stumbling over the Messiah means riches for the Gentiles, what will their inclusion mean if not something even better (Rom. 11:7–14)? In fact, when they do respond, it will be a miracle on a par with resurrection from the dead (Rom. 11:15). For if God can graft unnatural branches (Gentiles) into a tree, how much more can he graft in natural branches (Israel) that were temporarily cut off?

Paul expresses the hope that the hardening of Israel is temporary, and once the appointed number of Gentiles experience salvation, then, he says 'all Israel will be saved' (Rom. 11:26). Here 'all Israel' could mean (1) the church consisting of Jews and Gentiles, (2) a remnant of Jews, or (3) all the Jewish people. I think (2) is the most plausible, since it fits with the remnant theology of Romans 9–11 and with the focus on the fate of national Israel. A hope for a significant number of Jews to convert to Christ is what Paul looks forward to in the future, but he does not project the event all the way forward to the final tribulation, nor does he think it will be the trigger for the second or third coming of Christ (as in dispensational theology). For God's faithfulness to be vindicated and for Christians to have a true sense of assurance in God's saving righteousness, there needs to be a fitting end to God's dealings with Israel, or else God's own character is jeopardized and brought into question.[6]

---

6. On Paul and Israel see W. S. Campbell, 'Israel', in *DPL*, ed. G. F. Hawthorne, R. P. Martin and D. G. Reid (Downers Grove and Leicester: IVP, 1993), pp. 441–446; and on how Paul redefines the meaning of Israel's election see N. T. Wright, *Paul: Fresh Perspectives* (London: SPCK, 2005), pp. 108–129.

Parousia: game over, dude

The return of Christ means game, set and match, thank you ball-
boys and ballgirls, targets down and patch out, Elvis has left the
building and the fat lady is halfway through her second aria . . . Or,
as C. S. Lewis said, when the author of the play steps onto the
stage, you know the play is over.

Paul uses a variety of terms to describe this momentous event.
The Greek word *parousia* means literally 'presence' or 'arrival',
much like the royal visit of a king or dignitary to a provincial city
(1 Cor. 15:23; 1 Thess. 2:19; 3:13; 4:15; 5:23; 2 Thess. 2:1).
Epiphaneia means 'manifestation' or 'appearance', and it is used
both of the incarnation (2 Tim. 1:10) and of Christ's second
advent (2 Thess. 2:8; 1 Tim. 6:14; 2 Tim. 4:1, 8; Tit. 2:13; cf. Col.
3:4). *Apokalypsis*, another term used, is translatable as 'revelation'
or 'revealing', and signifies the divine disclosure of the Lord Jesus
(1 Cor. 1:7; 2 Thess. 1:7). By far the most frequent description is
that of the 'Day' of Jesus Christ (1 Cor. 1:8; 5:5; 2 Cor 1:14; Phil.
1:6, 10; 2:16; 2 Thess. 1:10; 2 Tim. 1:18), which evidently relates to
the 'Day of the Lord' in the Old Testament (e.g Amos 5:18; Isa.
2:12–22).

The return of Christ will mean the final and full manifestation
of the kingdom of God, and signals the dissolution of the old age.
Jesus returns to reign and rule, and every knee in all of creation
bows down before him. It is the hour when he will be by might
what he is by right. In the words of I. Howard Marshall, 'The language of parousia affirms that God acts through Jesus at the
consummation (as in creation and redemption) and that consummation means the submission of the fallen world to its Lord, the
final establishment of that lordship which was proclaimed through
resurrection.'[7]

Several events, including resurrection, are associated with the
parousia. Instantaneous with Christ's return is the general resurrection (1 Thess. 4:16; 1 Cor. 15:52). This is the moment when

7. I. H. Marshall, *1 and 2 Thessalonians*, NCB (Grand Rapids: Eerdmans, 1983),
p. 144.

Jesus Christ 'will transform our lowly bodies so that they will be like his glorious body' (Phil. 3:21). The question of the type of body that believers will receive was a burning question at Corinth, and Paul argues that the resurrection body is both continuous and discontinuous from our present state of existence and is a transphysical body of some kind (1 Cor. 15:35–50). The new body will be imperishable, glorious and powerful (1 Cor. 15:42–43).

What is perhaps more controversial (and I propose this view with a degree of hesitation) is that Paul also implies a messianic or millennial reign of Christ upon the earth. He states, 'But each in his own order: Christ the first fruits [is raised], *then* at his coming those who belong to Christ [will be raised]. *Then* the end, when he hands over the kingdom to God the Father when he has destroyed all dominion, authority and power. *For* it is necessary that he reigns until he has put all his enemies under his feet' (1 Cor. 15:23–25). There are three distinct stages: (1) Christ's resurrection, (2) the resurrection of believers at the parousia, and then (3) the 'end'. An interval is implied between Christ's resurrection and his parousia, and another interval between Christ's parousia and his subjugation of all authorities at the 'end'. The explanatory clause 'for' (*gar*) of verse 25 appears to make the reign of Christ temporally prior to the 'end' (*telos*) in verse 24. In other words, before the 'end' or the consummation is the reign of Christ over all authorities. I wouldn't bet my house on this one, but it is plausible, it fits the text and the idea comports with the millennial imagery we have in Revelation 20:1–10. Several Jewish apocalypses such as *4 Ezra* 7 and *2 Baruch* 29 also envisaged a messianic kingdom, and many early Christian interpreters, including Papias, Justin Martyr and Tertullian, looked forward to the millennial reign of Christ upon the earth.

The day of Christ is also to be a day of judgment for both believers and unbelievers. The idea of a future judgment of the righteous and the wicked was common in Jewish thought about the end of the age (cf. Rom. 2:12–16). For Paul, remember, the future age has already begun in part with Jesus' resurrection and the giving of the Spirit. God's verdict against sin has been executed in Christ's death and his verdict of vindication has been enacted in

Christ's resurrection.[8] The Day of Judgment holds no fear for Christians, then, because they have already heard in the gospel and experienced in the life of the Spirit the verdict, which is not condemnation but justification, not death but life (Rom. 8:1, 33–34). In fact, the only one who can condemn them is at the very moment interceding for them (Rom. 8:34). Still, Paul maintains that servants of God will have their ministries evaluated for what they truly are (1 Cor. 3:10–15). All believers will also stand before the judgment seat of Christ (2 Cor. 5:10; Rom. 14:10). Paul can make some graphic and sombre warnings to Christians about what will happen to them if they do not continue in faith and if they sow to the flesh and give themselves over to sin (e.g. Rom. 8:13; 1 Cor. 6:9–10; Gal. 5:21). The only saving faith is persevering faith, and although nobody is saved by works, works nonetheless demonstrate the integrity of the faith we profess.

One of the most glorious descriptions of the new creation comes from Romans 8. There, Paul personifies creation itself as burgeoning with expectation as it 'eagerly waits for the revelation of the sons of God' (Rom. 8:19). In other words, the created order itself is desperately longing for the resurrection of the children of God because it knows that it is next in line for its own resurrection, where the entire cosmos will be created anew. Paul adds that 'creation itself will also be freed from the slavery of corruption into the glorious freedom of the children of God' (Rom. 8:21). The freedom from decay and the everlasting glory experienced by believers at their resurrection will eventually spill over to creation, which will share in a similar freedom and glory soon after. In much the same way as creation 'groans' for such things, so do Christians in the meantime, as they wait for the redemption of their bodies (and not redemption *from* their bodies as in Gnostic thought). It is this hope for resurrection and new creation that sustains believers, and they wait for it patiently and prayerfully as led by God's Spirit (Rom. 8:22–27).

---

8. M. Seifrid, *Christ, our Righteousness*, NSBT 9 (Leicester: Apollos; Downers Grove: IVP, 2000).

Personal eschatology

What happens to believers when they die before the parousia? This was a question Paul encountered more than once (1 Thess. 4:13–18; 1 Cor. 15:29–30, 51), and he had contemplated the prospect of his own departure before the Lord's return (Phil. 1:20–26; 1 Cor. 6:14; 2 Tim. 4:6). There clearly is an afterlife, according to Paul. He refers to a hope stored up for believers in heaven (Col. 1:5), the promise of life and eternal life (Rom. 5:21; 6:22–23; Gal. 6:8; 2 Cor. 5:4; 1 Tim. 1:16; 4:8; 6:12; 2 Tim. 1:1; Tit. 1:2; 3:7); as per Revelation, there is the 'Book of Life' (Phil. 4:3), and he says that if this life is all there is to hope for, then believers are the most pitiable of people (1 Cor. 15:19).

While Paul's main hope is for resurrection from the dead (Rom. 8:11; Phil. 3:10–12; 1 Thess. 4:16; 1 Cor. 6:14; 15:1–58; 2 Cor. 4:14; cf. Col. 3:4), yet ahead of that event he can say that at death believers put on a heavenly 'dwelling from God' (2 Cor. 5:1) and go to be 'with Christ, which is better by far' (Phil. 1:23). In the final days of World War Two, Dietrich Bonhoeffer was hanged with piano wire by the Gestapo for his part in the plot to assassinate Hitler. His final words were reported to have been 'This is the end, but for me, the beginning.' The same is true of those who die in Christ – and what a glorious beginning it is!

8. ONE GOD, ONE LORD: MONOTHEISM AND THE MESSIAH

When I was a youngster, Jehovah's Witnesses rarely came to our house. My mother scared them off with colourful expressions indigenous to Australia, which made it crystal clear they were not welcome! I also remember that a house not far from ours had an amusing sign in the front yard that said, 'Jehovah's Witnesses Beware! Our Dog is Islamic.' However, if you want to repel the arguments of Jehovah's Witnesses that Jesus is not God, you do not need profane language or a 120 pound Doberman named 'Mohammed'. All you need is the apostle Paul, who is utterly convinced that Jesus participates in the identity of God.[1]

In the writings of early Christianity, we encounter a unique phenomenon: the Christians were for the most part genuine monotheists, that is, they believed there is only one God who is the Creator and who has made a covenant with Israel. Paul himself was a monotheist, as a cursory reading of Romans makes clear. At

---

1. This theme is explored more fully in R. Bauckham, *God Crucified: Monotheism and Christology in the New Testament* (Carlisle: Paternoster, 1998).

the same time, the early Christians, including Paul, believed that Jesus Christ was to be identified with God. In the words of Francis Watson, 'If . . . God is, finally and ultimately, not just provisionally and in passing – the God who raised Jesus our Lord from the dead, the God and Father of our Lord Jesus Christ, then God's own identity is determined by the relation to Jesus just as Jesus' identity is determined by the relation to God.'[2]

Amazingly, there is a remarkable overlap between the functions of God and Jesus in creation and redemption. Equally astounding is that honorific titles like 'Lord' are used to refer to both Jesus and the Father in Paul's writings. When authors like Paul mentioned God, they felt constrained to tie in Jesus too, and whenever Paul mentioned Jesus, he was likewise compelled to mention God in the same breath.[3] Paul is an advocate of what we should call *messianic monotheism*,[4] that is, God is known through Jesus the Messiah, or Jesus is the one who reveals and manifests the person and work of God. I want to examine several texts briefly that demonstrate the presence of this sentiment in Paul's letters (there is not enough space here to cover every text).

The Corinthian letters

In the Corinthian correspondence are several points where Paul, almost in passing, intimates a close relationship between Jesus and God. The most basic creed or confession of Israel was the Shema of Deuteronomy that set forth Israel's faith as an exclusively monotheistic faith. And yet in 1 Corinthians 8:6, Paul echoes the Shema in his teaching about different 'gods' and 'lords', applying it in relation to Christ.

---

2. F. B. Watson, 'The Triune Divine Identity', *JSNT* 80 (2000), p. 117.

3. M. de Jonge, *God's Final Envoy: Early Christology and Jesus' Own View of His Mission* (Grand Rapids: Eerdmans, 1998), p. 130.

4. Cf. similarly, N. T. Wright, *The Climax of the Covenant* (Edinburgh: T. & T. Clark, 1991), p. 114; *Paul: Fresh Perspectives* (London: SPCK, 2005), pp. 91–96.

Deuteronomy 6:4	1 Corinthians 8:6
Hear O Israel!	[Y]et for us there is
The Lord our *God*,	*one God*, the Father, from whom are all things and for whom we live,
the *Lord* is *one*.	*one Lord* Jesus Christ, through whom are all things and through whom we live.

Paul does not say that 'Jesus is the Father' (tantamount to what would later be called the heresy of 'modalism'), but sets the identity of Jesus within the framework of the Shema, so that the titles 'Lord' and 'God' can equally describe Jesus and the Father.

At the end of 1 Corinthians, Paul closes the letter with a short exhortation: 'If anyone does not love the Lord let him be accursed. *Our Lord, come!*' (1 Cor. 16:22). That final phrase 'Our Lord, come!' is transliterated from the Aramaic *marana tha*, where *mara* stands for 'Lord' or 'Yahweh' (*kyrios* in the Septuagint). Paul arguably mimics a praise or prayer from the Aramaic-speaking church, which in effect regarded the future coming of Jesus as the eschatological coming of God and used a designation for Jesus ordinarily used of God.

In 2 Corinthians 8, Paul exhorts the Corinthians to generosity in their giving by invoking the example of Jesus himself: 'For you know the grace of our Lord Jesus Christ, though he was rich, yet for your sakes he became poor, so that by his poverty you might become rich' (2 Cor. 8:9). The transition from riches to poverty clearly points to a theology of incarnation. In becoming human, Jesus 'became poor'. Note also that the incarnation was for a salvific purpose: Jesus 'became poor' (took on human form) so that the Corinthians might 'become rich' (experience salvation).

Philippians and Colossians

The captivity epistles include some incredibly rich, vibrant and elaborate descriptions of Christ. The well-known Christ hymn of Philippians 2:5–11 (see more on this in chapter 9 below) is an excellent example of Paul's articulation of messianic monotheism. The hymn, or poetic prose, is fundamentally an ethical exhortation towards humility and self-giving rather than comprising an exercise in Christological speculation. Even so, Paul still draws on language and imagery that unmistakably places Jesus in the orbit of the divine identity and intimates the reality and purpose of his incarnation:

> Have this in mind with one another, which is that in Christ Jesus:
>
>> Who, being in the form of God,
>>> he did not consider equality with God to consist of grasping;
>> Rather, he poured himself out
>>> by taking the form of a servant,
>>> being made in human likeness
>>> and being found in appearance as a man.
>> He humbled himself and become obedient to death
>>> even death on a cross!
>> Therefore, God exalted him and graciously gave him the name that is above every name
>>> in order that at the name of Jesus every knee should bow
>>> in heaven, on the earth, and under the earth
>>> and every tongue confess
>>> that Jesus Christ is Lord to the glory of God the Father.

What we have in this passage is an important window into the worship and theological reflection of the early church. If the hymn was not itself composed by Paul but derived from Greek-speaking Christians in Damascus or Antioch, then we can say that a Christology of messianic monotheism emerged very early on and even precedes Paul. I want to identify four main thoughts in this passage.

First, 'being in the form of God' is a reference to the characteristics of deity, and the same is true of 'equality with God'. In other words, Jesus possessed the nature and prerogatives of God. The transition from 'form of God' to 'form of a servant' implies a gracious condescension on the part of Christ Jesus in becoming human. It is moreover a voluntary act undertaken out of obedience to the Father. Thus, even in the Godhead there is equality in being with subordination in roles.

Second, the phrase 'did not consider equality with God to consist of grasping' is difficult to translate and interpret (see the AV, which renders it 'thought it not robbery to be equal with God'). Tom Wright hits the nail on the head in his summary of verses 6–8: 'The pre-existent son regarded equality with God not as excusing him from the task of (redemptive) suffering and death, but actually as uniquely qualifying him for that vocation.'[5]

Third, theologians have endlessly debated what exactly it was that Jesus emptied himself of: his glory, his independent exercise of divine prerogatives, certain attributes like omniscience and so on. This entire debate, however, is misdirected. Jesus' self-emptying did not consist of laying aside any one of his divine attributes or putting aside his equal authority with God: more likely, it is a general statement of his self-giving attitude. In contrast to 'grasping' or 'seizing' for one's own advantage, Christ Jesus was self-giving and 'poured himself out' by taking the form of a servant.[6] The important thing is not *what* he poured out but *how* he did so, and the answer is of course his incarnation and going to the cross.

Fourth, verses 9–11 are a clear echo of Isaiah 45:23.

Philippians 2:9–11	Isaiah 45:23
Therefore, God exalted him and graciously gave him the name that is above every name in order that at the name of Jesus every knee should bow in heaven, on the earth, and under the earth and every tongue confess that Jesus Christ is Lord to the glory of God the Father.	By myself I have sworn; from my mouth has gone out in righteousness a word that shall not return: 'To me every knee shall bow, every tongue shall swear allegiance.'

This is a crystal-clear statement that Paul regards Jesus as participating in the divine identity. He takes the language normally used

5. Wright, *Climax of the Covenant*, pp. 83–84.

6. G. D. Fee, *Paul's Letter to the Philippians*, NICNT (Grand Rapids: Eerdmans, 1995), pp. 210–211.

to describe Yahweh or 'the Lord' and applies it to Jesus. When the Jehovah's Witnesses come to my door (without my mother in the house I actually get a crack at them nowadays), I always take them to Isaiah 45:23 and ask, 'Who is the prophet talking about?' The answer is of course Jehovah or Yahweh. I then take them to Philippians 2:9–11 and ask, 'Who is Paul talking about?' The answers vary and I shall not go into the details; suffice it to say, I have not yet convinced any Jehovah's Witnesses, but maybe one day, Lord willing.

My favourite passage in my favourite book of the entire New Testament is Colossians 1:15–20, which reads:

> He is the image of the invisible God,
> the firstborn over all of creation,
>> because in him all things were created
>> in the heavens and upon the earth,
>> whether visible or invisible,
>> whether thrones or lords,
>> whether rulers or authorities,
>> all things were created through him and for him.
> And he is before all things
>> and in him all things are sustained.
> And he is the head of the body, the church.
> He is the beginning,
> the firstborn from among the dead,
>> in order that he might have the supremacy in all things,
>> because in him [God] was pleased to have all his fullness dwell,
>> and through him to reconcile to himself all things,
>> by making peace through his blood shed on the cross [through him],
>> whether things on the earth or whether things in the heavens.

What is extraordinary about this text is that the roles of creation and redemption, roles ordinarily associated with God, are here predicated of Jesus. The mention of 'firstborn' does not mean that Jesus is a created being. It has its background in the Old Testament, as Israel was also known as God's firstborn son (Exod. 4:22), and the same title could be used of Israel's monarch (Ps. 89:27). Furthermore, in families of antiquity the firstborn was the appointed heir who held a privilege of rank in the execution of a will.

To refer to Jesus as the 'firstborn over all of creation', then, is to speak of his sovereignty over creation and his pre-eminent authority over the human race. He possesses supremacy in terms of both time and rank, pre-existence and pre-eminence. In fact, Paul also says that Jesus is the sustaining force of the universe: he is the reason why there is a cosmos instead of a chaos. Jesus provides the intergalactic glue that holds the universe together and is that which physicists have spent the last fifty years looking for, namely a 'theory of everything'.[7]

The work of salvation is also uniquely ascribed to Jesus. He is the firstborn from among the dead. That is, Jesus' resurrection is simultaneously the prototype and the promise of the resurrection of believers. God's new age has exploded among the current order of corruption and death and brings the life of heaven to earth as a foretaste of what is to come. Additionally, the fullness of God dwells not in statues or in idols but in his firstborn Son, who is Creator of all and Captain of the new creation. The work of cosmic reconciliation takes place through the blood of his cross, where he also disarms oppressive spiritual powers and even leaves them in disarray (see Col. 2:15). That was a momentous claim to make in a world proudly pluralistic and polytheistic. The adding of gods to the Roman pantheon was a clever way of ensuring the peace, because peoples, nations and tribes would be less likely to rebel if they did not know which side the gods would be on. As such, the Christian claim that Jesus is the archetype representation of God or the 'image of God' (see also 2 Cor. 4:4) who brooks no rivals was regarded as needlessly intolerant towards others and potentially disruptive to the thin veneer of peace and social stability Roman power imposed.

Celsus, a pagan writer in the second century, wrote a vicious attack on the exclusive claims of Christians: 'It makes no

---

7. The term 'a theory of everything' is taken from physicists and cosmologists who hope to discover a grand scientific theory that will explain everything about the origins and existence of the universe.

difference if one invokes the highest God or Zeus or Adonai or Sabaoth or Amoun, as the Egyptians do, or Papaios as the Scythians do' (Origen, *Cels.* 5.41). The poet Alexander Pope (1688–1744) rehearsed the same thought when he said:

> Father of all, in every age
> In every clime, adored
> By saint, by savage, or by sage,
> Jehovah, Jove or Lord.[8]

Though Christians were denounced as atheists and as threats to the public order, the majority of the orthodox Christians maintained the uniqueness of Christ as God's agent in creation and redemption. If there are other so-called gods, then Jesus is sovereign over them. If there are lesser lords of a religious kind, then Jesus is pre-eminent above them. As the heir of the cosmos, nothing is beyond the purview of his authority and the reach of his reign, for the entire created order was set in motion not only *by him* but also *for him*.

Galatians and Romans

In several places in his other letters, Paul mentions, if only in passing, something of the scope of Jesus' mission and the nature of his identity. Both Galatians 4:4 and Romans 8:3 refer to his being 'sent' by God the Father:

Galatians 4:4–5	*Romans 8:3*
But when the time had fully come, *God sent out his Son*, born of a woman, born under the law, to redeem those under the law.	For what the law was powerless to do in that it was weakened by the flesh, *God did by sending his own Son* in the likeness of sinful flesh to be a sin offering.

---

8. A. Pope, 'The Universal Prayer', stanza 1.

The Jewish perspective of course was that God had sent his law to Israel, and the law was said to be the pre-existent embodiment of God's wisdom and not just something he had made up at Sinai. Later, God sends his Son in similar fashion and the two texts lend themselves equally to the idea of pre-existence. Whereas God initially sent the law, now he sends the Son to redeem those under the law by being a sin offering for their transgression of the law.

There is one other place in Romans where Paul may well make mention of Jesus' divine identity. That verse is Romans 9:5 which, unfortunately, is grammatically ambiguous as to whether or not it states that Jesus is God. Note the contrast between two different translations:

RSV	ESV
To them belong the patriarchs, and of their race, according to the flesh, is the Christ. *God who is over all* be blessed for ever. Amen.	To them belong the patriarchs, and from their race, according to the flesh, *is the Christ who is God over all,* blessed forever. Amen.

The problem is that the earliest manuscripts were written in block capital letters with no spaces between words and no punctuation. So the question of how to punctuate the English translation requires not just a translation but also an interpretation. To put it simply, does the concluding clause, which literally reads, 'the one being overall God blessed into the age amen' refer to God (RSV) or to Christ (ESV)? Some doubt that Paul could or would make such a clear and unqualified reference to Christ's deity and point out that the grammar is far from clear. With that caveat in mind, I lean towards the second option, that it refers to Christ as God, because (1) the natural antecedent for 'the one being overall' is 'Christ', (2) the flow of thought seems to be that the Messiah is a descendant from Israel and also the God of Israel, (3) Pauline doxologies usually run 'blessed be God' rather than 'God be blessed', and (4) the reference to Jesus as God is not out of order with what Paul says of Christ elsewhere, such as 1 Corinthians 8:6, 15:47, 16:22 and Philippians 2:5–11.

Conclusion

I once heard the story of a missionary travelling on a train in India who met a man who regarded Christians as exceedingly dogmatic in their view of God. The man was even able to cite Scripture to back up his claim and referred our missionary friend to Isaiah 64:4, which Paul himself quotes in 1 Corinthians 2:9: 'No eye has seen, no ear has heard, no heart has conceived what God has prepared for those who love him.' Therefore, if God is so mysterious and indescribable, it is arrogant and wrong-headed to be so dogmatic about what we claim to know about him. Yet our missionary friend also knew the context of Paul's quote and cited the following verse from 1 Corinthians 2:10: 'but God has revealed it to us by his Spirit'.

God is indeed mysterious, but in Christ Jesus the mystery has been unravelled for us. In fact, the entire context of 1 Corinthians 2:1–16 is a stunning exposition of the Christian knowledge of God as he is known through the word of the cross and the illuminating work of the Spirit. Paul does not picture himself as groping in vain after a definition of God or trying to come up with a vague description of a god who is the impersonal expression of some ultimate reality hidden behind the game of language. For Paul, God is known in the grace of the Lord Jesus Christ, in the love of the Father and in fellowship with the Holy Spirit.

9. LIVING A LIFE WORTHY OF THE GOSPEL: THE ETHICS OF PAUL

Paul is no doctrinaire theologian and his interests pertain to far more than making sure his converts have the right set of beliefs about justification, eschatology, the sacraments and politics. Truth undoubtedly matters to Paul, but he is also deeply concerned about the behaviour, actions, attitudes and lifestyle of the churches. He wants to know what kind of people they were, what kind of community they have become and, most of all, whether they are fulfilling their calling in Christ Jesus. To use Paul's own words, he wants to make sure they are living a life 'worthy of the gospel of Christ' (Phil. 1:27), both individually and corporately.

The issue of exactly how to live such a life is a pressing dilemma for the following reasons:

1. Although the Corinthian Christians are numbered among those 'being saved' (1 Cor. 1:18; 2 Cor. 2:15), they still struggle against the sinful impulses of the world, the flesh and the devil.
2. They have to confront the problem of how to live in a pagan city without reflecting the values and decadence of a pagan society.

3. They are confronted with the problem of how to differentiate between areas of conviction and areas of command. This is especially acute in Jewish–Gentile congregations, where people have very different ideas about how to live a God-pleasing life and about which parts of the Mosaic law continue into the new age inaugurated by Christ and the Spirit.

Thus, what we shall look at in this chapter is Paul's ethics and how, according to Paul, God's people are to live.

The new has come

The new creation promised in Isaiah (65:17; 66:22) is coming, and the first instalment has already come in the spiritual rebirth of the followers of the Lord Jesus Christ. Paul writes to the Corinthians, 'So then, if anyone is in Christ, he is a new creation, the old has passed away, and behold, the new has come!' (2 Cor. 5:17). According to Paul, the fact that Christ died *for them* and the accompanying fact that they have also died *with Christ* mean that a fundamental shift has taken place in their identity. One implication Paul makes from this is that ethnicity is no longer determinative for their identity, because 'neither circumcision counts for anything, nor uncircumcision, but a *new creation*' (Gal. 6:15; cf. 3:28; 5:6; 1 Cor. 7:19; Col. 3:11), and this has radical repercussions for the life of the Christian community.

Paul also teaches that Christians are, paradoxically, dead and reborn, crucified and resurrected, wasting away and being renewed (e.g. 2 Cor. 4:7–18). By virtue of their union with Christ and their possession of the Spirit, they are not who they were before; instead, they are now 'in Christ' and 'of Christ'. In their final end state, this new creation will result in believers being conformed to the image of the Son of God (Rom. 8:29; 2 Cor. 3:18). That renewal is on the one hand a reality, but is something they are also commanded to pursue and practice. Which is why Paul says in Romans, 'Do not be conformed to this age, but be transformed by the renewing of your minds' (Rom. 12:2), that is, to live as part of the new creation even though it is not here in its fullness. Colossians and Ephesians speak of putting off the 'old man' and putting on, or clothing oneself in, the 'new man', which is treated as a present reality (Col. 3:9–10) and something to be performed time and again (Eph. 4:22–24).

I have found it common in sermons for preachers to say that Christians have two natures, spiritual and carnal, and then to liken these two natures to fighting dogs. Our duty, so it goes, is to ensure that we feed one dog and starve the other. But this is not quite true, since Christians have *one* true nature: the new creation. The process of sanctification (growth in holiness, godliness and love) is about becoming who and what we truly are, cracked vessels that have been transformed into precious vases. When sin affects Christians, it is not because a civil war is raging within our bodies and we have somehow temporarily yielded to our carnal as opposed to spiritual nature (this is based on a bad reading of Rom. 7). Instead, it is more like we have failed to *be* and *act* as we truly are: new creations. A better analogy to use in order to exhort Christians to stop indulging in sin is perhaps more along the lines of urging us to stop trying to play LPs on a CD player: play CDs on a CD player. Stop trying to load old software onto new hardware. Be what we are, be what we are becoming, and be what we will be on the final day of Christ Jesus![1]

Because of this, do that!

Paul's exhortation to righteousness and holiness normally takes the form of 'Because of this, do that!' This is called the *indicative* and the *imperative* of Pauline ethics.[2] Spelled out, it means Paul's ethical instruction is rooted in the prior act of salvation God has

---

1. After writing this sentence, I came across an excellent exposition of the same point by T. R. Schreiner, *Paul: Apostle of God's Glory in Christ: A Pauline Theology* (Leicester: Apollos, 2001), pp. 254–255.
2. See the explanation and qualification of this description in J. D. G. Dunn, *The Theology of Paul the Apostle* (Edinburgh: T. & T. Clark, 1998), pp. 626–631.

wrought in Christ. Paul's appeal goes along the lines of 'Christ died and rose to reconcile you to God (indicative), therefore, do away with sin and do righteousness (imperative).' Here are several examples from the apostle's letters:

> Therefore, we were buried with him through baptism into death, so that just as Christ was raised from the dead through the glory of the Father, we too might walk in newness of life.
>
> (Rom. 6:4)

> Therefore, I exhort you, brothers and sisters, by the mercies of God, to present your bodies as living sacrifices, holy and pleasing to God, which is your rational worship.
>
> (Rom. 12:1)

> Clean out the old yeast in order that you may be a new batch, as you already are unleavened. For our paschal lamb, Christ, has been sacrificed. So then, let us celebrate the festival, not with the old yeast, the yeast of malice and evil, but with the unleavened bread of sincerity and truth.
>
> (1 Cor. 5:7–8)

> Or do you not know that your body is a temple of the Holy Spirit within you, which you have from God? And that you are not your own, for you were bought with a price, therefore, honour God with your body.
>
> (1 Cor. 6:19–20)

The very structure of Paul's letters often exhibits this framework of the indicative and imperative. Romans 1 – 5, Colossians 1 – 2 and Ephesians 1 – 3 focus on the gift of *salvation* given in Christ, while Romans 6 – 8, Colossians 3 – 4 and Ephesians 4 – 6 focus on *appropriating* that gift through living holy lives in a pagan world.[3] The link between the indicative and the imperative is not merely a logical one; it is rooted in the power of the new creation that believers experience and the life of the Spirit they partake of. In

---

3. Eph. 2:8–10 is the single passage that demonstrates this pattern the most lucidly.

other words, God provides the resources for Christians to do what he commands.

Consider this exhortation from Philippians: 'Therefore, my beloved friends, just as you have always obeyed me, not only in my presence, but much more now in my absence, work out your own salvation with fear and trembling; for it is God who is at work within you, enabling you both to will and to work for his good pleasure' (Phil. 2:12–13). In context 'work out your own salvation with fear and trembling' is a paraphrase for remaining obedient to the pattern of Paul's teaching, and the enabling factor is that God 'is at work within you'. Thus, Paul is not in the business of offering self-help moralism and telling Christians just to try harder than other people at being good persons. The charge to produce good works and to sow seeds of righteousness cannot be separated from the continuing and sustaining relationship the Christian has with God.

To give another example, the Corinthians are perhaps the most worldly and untransformed bunch of Jesus-followers in the early church, and yet the apostle says to them, 'He [God] will sustain you until the end, so that you will be blameless on the day of our Lord Jesus Christ. God is faithful, by whom you were called into the fellowship of his Son, Jesus Christ our Lord' (1 Cor. 1:8–9). Left to their own devices, this regenerate lot will easily degenerate into just another club in Corinth, since they are anything but 'blameless'. However, Paul knows that God wants to confirm them on the final day of history, and until then his Spirit is working in them to transform them gradually to the point where their moral state will befit the titles of 'saints', 'sons' and 'chosen ones' God has conferred on them. There can be no obviating of personal responsibility to put sin to death and to hunger for holiness, but those imperatives exist only in a relationship with God, a relationship sustained by grace and empowered by the Spirit.

No longer under law, but under grace

When Gentiles became proselytes to Judaism, they were ordinarily expected to take up the obligation to follow the law of Moses. Paul, however, rejected this measure for Gentiles who had come to faith in Jesus as the Messiah. But why did the apostle disregard the law as a mandatory requirement for Gentile converts on admission to the church, and what did he think would prevent them from reverting to their pagan ways if not the divinely given commandments of the Torah?

The weakness of the law

One of the most perplexing topics in Pauline studies is Paul's understanding of the law as it relates to Christians.[4] Galatians seems to engage in a volatile polemic against the law, while Romans is far more positive and almost apologetic in its qualified recognition of the law's place in redemptive history despite its weaknesses. So what is wrong with the law and what continuing role does the law have in the life of the Christian?

In Galatians 3 – 4, Romans 6 – 8, 10 and 2 Corinthians 3, Paul provides his most concise explanation of the weakness of the law. In two places (Gal. 3:12; Rom. 10:5) he quotes Leviticus 18:5: 'The one who does these things [obeys the law] will live by them,' but due to disobedience the law brings curses instead of life. In 2 Corinthians 3:6, he says, 'the letter kills, but the Spirit gives life'.[5] The law is bound up with the old age and is part of a triangle of forces consisting of law–sin–death, a triangle that brings condemnation on both Jews and Gentiles. Moreover, since the law was the national charter for Israel, it also meant that blessings and salvation were limited to Israel. But this was temporary, and God's original plan given through Abraham was to reach all nations. Hence, according to Paul, the Mosaic law has three main functions:

1. *To highlight the holiness of God and the severity of sin.* The decrees of the law, therefore, enabled God's people to realize they lived in a moral universe before a God who was not morally indifferent,

---

4. See F. Thielman, *Paul and the Law: A Contextual Approach* (Downers Grove: IVP, 1994).

5. The great theologian Augustine regarded Romans as an exposition of this point.

and they had been chosen to reflect the glory of God in the presence of the nations through the covenantal life of their community (Rom. 2:2–4, 17–24; 3:5–8, 19–20; 7:7–13; Gal. 2:16).

2. *To be a temporary administration of God's grace to govern his people.* It functioned to set them apart from the nations and to cocoon God's promises around them for a time, until the promised seed of Abraham (Jesus Christ) had come, the one who would bring the Gentiles into God's covenant family (Gal. 3:15–25; 4:1–7; Rom. 10:4).

3. *To foreshadow and introduce the coming of Jesus Christ.* When he came, he would save people from the condemnation of the law (Rom. 3:21–22; 1 Cor. 5:7; 10:3; Col. 2:17).

As such, the law can *condemn* but it cannot *redeem* (Gal. 2:21); it can highlight sin and sensuality but it cannot restrain them (Col. 2:23). What the law could not do, God did by sending his Son and his Spirit so that sinful Jews and Gentiles could both be accounted righteous before him and live righteously for him (Gal. 4:4–6). What Paul so wonderfully expounds in Romans 6 is that, by dying with Christ, believers have died to sin and the law, and now live in the newness of life Christ ushered in. Thus, (1) *possession* of the law, with its distinctive practices of circumcision, Sabbath-keeping and dietary laws, no longer marks out God's elect, (2) *performance* of the law cannot and will not be the basis of vindication at the day of judgment, and (3) *practice* of the law is no longer the definitive charter for the life of the new-covenant people.

Instead, these things are replaced by faith and faithfulness in Christ. If that is true, then Paul anticipates a possible objection: 'Shall we go on sinning so that grace may increase?' (Rom. 6:1). How, without the law, does one stop new Christians from acting like old pagans? Does the law have any significance for the life of the Christian community? To those questions we now turn. But before we do, let us take a brief look at Romans 7:

A note on Romans 7: law and sin
A passage frequently used to describe the struggle with sin in the life of the Christian is Romans 7:7–25. On many readings the 'I'

and 'wretched man' of Romans 7 is identified with Paul's autobio-
graphical portrait of himself, which is then applied to Christians in
their struggle with sin. Yet it is unclear who is being referred to,
and proposals include Adam, Israel, pre-conversion Paul, post-
conversion Paul or the average Christian.[6] Let me suggest a way
forward.

1. *Romans 7 must be understood in its context.* Paul anticipates a possible objection to his gospel, namely if the law is not a means of
salvation, no longer the definitive guide to righteous living, and not
the badge that marks out the people of God (the argument of
Rom. 3:21 – 6:23), then what was the purpose of the giving of the
law in the first place? In Romans 7, Paul sets out to answer this
objection, defending the place of the law in redemptive history.
He argues that the law is good and holy, but while it can *reveal* our
sin it cannot *release* us from it. Even worse, the law leads to sin,
which then brings death. Moreover, Christians are no longer under
law, because they have died to the law in the death of Christ. Paul
writes, 'but now we are released from the law' (Rom. 7:6), and
expounds this point in Romans 8:1–17, where he says the righteous requirements of the law are fulfilled by those who walk
according to the Spirit.

2. *The passage cannot refer to the pre-Christian Paul,* since we find no
evidence that Paul was tormented by the gravity of his sin and
anguished over his inability to find a gracious God. The pre-
Christian Paul knew that atonement was available through the
sacrificial system in the temple and, at any rate, in the letter to the
Philippians he apparently regarded himself as 'blameless', not
guilt stricken (Phil. 3:6). It was the preaching of the Puritans that
supposed one should preach law in order to show sinners how
wretched they were and thus drive them to Christ in want of
grace. Paul was not Puritan in this regard.

3. *Paul is not talking about post-conversion Christians in this section,*
since the statement 'I am of the flesh, sold under sin' (Rom. 7:14)

---

6. For a historical survey of the debate see M. Reasoner, *Romans in Full Circle:
   A History of Interpretation* (Louisville: Westminster John Knox, 2005),
   pp. 67–84.

conflicts with what he says about Christians in Romans 6, where
he declares that they have been freed from sin (Rom. 6:6–7, 17–18,
22). Those subject to the law struggle to obey it (Rom. 7:22, 25),
while Christians are free from the law (Rom. 6:14–15; 7:6).

4. *Paul is not talking explicitly about Adam*, since he appears to have
finished referring to Adam in Romans 5:12–21 and it is hard to
think of Adam as being under the stipulations of the Mosaic law
pertaining to covetousness (Rom. 7:7). Still, there are some
genuine parallels between Romans 7:7–25 and Genesis 2 – 3. For
instance 'sin . . . deceived me and through it killed me' (Rom. 7:11)
and 'The serpent deceived me, and I ate' (Gen. 3:13). This parallel
shows that the experience of the 'I' recapitulates the experience of
Adam in the garden of Eden. While Adam is not the focal point,
the narration refers to human beings who have discovered in
themselves the dark vestiges of the Adamic self.[7]

5. *The 'I' language of Romans 7:7–25 is very similar to some of the psalms
where the psalmist oscillates between the 'I/me' and 'Israel' (e.g. Pss 129, 130,
131).* Likewise, Romans 7:7–25 may be an example of *prosōpopoiia*, or
a speech-in-character that was a well-known rhetorical device in
Paul's day.[8] Thus, Paul seems to be speaking in the first person as
'Israel', and in passionate and powerful language highlights the
plight of the Jews under the law, the struggle with sin they faced
because of the law, and their inability to find salvation in the law.
However, this struggle is only apparent retrospectively from the
vantage point of faith in Christ.

For Paul's Roman audience, most of whom consist of Gentiles
who once had some level of attachment to the synagogue and
some degree of adherence to the Mosaic legislation, this imagery is
a persuasive justification for having a religious framework that
focuses on Christ rather than on the Torah. They can now, with the
benefit of hindsight, identify with the experience Paul narrates and
thereby more readily understand his polemic against the law. They
can also agree that Paul is not antinomian or promoting godless

---

7. L. E. Keck, *Romans*, ANTC (Nashville: Abingdon, 2005), p. 180.

8. D. E. Aune, *The New Testament in its Literary Environment* (Cambridge: James
Clark, 1987), p. 168.

behaviour, because he speaks of a righteousness based on life in the Spirit, rather than a righteousness based on life under the law.

In sum, I opt for a *pre-Christian* reading of Romans 7:7–25.

The fruitful life of the Christian

While Christians may not be under law, but under grace (Rom. 6:14–15), nonetheless, we belong to Christ in order to 'bear fruit to God' (Rom. 7:4) and be 'filled with the fruit of righteousness that comes through Jesus Christ' (Phil. 1:11). In other words, liberty from the law is not a licence for sin.

So where does the imperative come from in Paul's ethics? In short, it derives from four areas.

The example of Jesus Christ

A central ingredient in Paul's recipe for Christian ethics is the example of Jesus Christ. This is demonstrated most aptly in the sublime Christ hymn mentioned earlier, Philippians 2:5–11. In reflecting on this hymn, theologians debate what it meant for Jesus to be in the 'form of God', to have 'equality with God' (v. 5) and what Jesus 'emptied himself' of (v. 6). While this reflection is legitimate, it can obscure the main point of the hymn, which is ethical rather than Christological. The purpose of Philippians 2:5–11 is to extol the virtues of self-giving and self-debasement as a means of promoting harmonious relationships among the Christian community in Philippi.

In contrast to 'grasping' or 'seizing' for one's own advantage, Christ was self-giving and 'poured himself out' by taking the form of a servant: the model believers should strive to emulate. Another instance of this is Romans 5:12–21, where Jesus, as the second Adam, is obedient and faithful towards God, whereas the first Adam was disobedient and faithless. While the 'one act of righteousness' Jesus committed as the second Adam results in justifying life for those who are in the first Adam (Rom. 5:17–18), Jesus' obedience is also paradigmatic and exemplary and results in others being 'constituted as righteous' through connection with the new Adam (Rom. 5:19).

The motif of imitating the example of Christ is spread

throughout Paul's letters. In terms of *generosity*, Paul urges the Corinthians, 'For you know the grace of our Lord Jesus Christ, though he was rich, yet for your sake he became poor, so that by his poverty you might become rich' (2 Cor. 8:9). In regard to *hospitality*, he says to the Romans, 'welcome one another as Christ has welcomed you' (Rom. 15:7). In reference to *reconciliation*, Paul exhorts the Colossians to 'forgive each other, just as the Lord has forgiven you' (Col. 3:13).

Paul even asks the Corinthians to imitate him, since he is an imitator of Christ (1 Cor. 11:1). A point of order, however, is required here, as Paul is not urging Christians to imitate Jesus as if they were imitating a great philosopher like Socrates or a celebrated rabbi like Gamaliel. Jesus was no mere sage or wise man who established a twelve-step programme for holy living. The example Paul speaks of pertains to the covenant God incarnated in the person of Jesus; and this Jesus is also the substitute and Saviour of believers through his sacrificial death on the cross. While Jesus' life and death are unique in their character and effect, they are also the model believers are to follow (see 1 Pet. 2:21–24). Thus, and this is crucial, as God is towards us in Christ, so are we Christians to be towards others.

The teaching of Jesus

While isolated quotes (e.g. 1 Cor. 7:10) and certain echoes of the Jesus tradition (e.g. Rom. 14:14) (see chapters 1 and 3 above) can be found in Paul's letters, for the most part there is a paucity of references to what Jesus taught. This is explainable on the grounds that the issues Paul encountered, such as circumcision, criteria for apostleship, and how to facilitate Jew–Gentile fellowship did not feature much as part of Jesus' teaching in Galilee and Judea. His passing reference to the 'word of Christ' (Col. 3:16) could denote the teaching about Christ or the teaching from Christ, but it is impossible to determine. More fruitful ground for uncovering Jesus' pattern of instruction in Paul's letters is from his reference to the 'law of Christ':

> Bear one another's burdens, and in this way you will fulfil the law of Christ.
>
> (Gal. 6:2)

To those outside the law I became as one outside the law (though I am
not free from God's law but am accountable under Christ's law) so that I
might win the lawless.

(1 Cor. 9:21)

But what is the law of Christ? Is it the Mosaic law reloaded and
rebooted with its proper interpretation? Bruce Longenecker maintains that the law of Christ is 'the Mosaic law that comes to its
fullest and proper expression in the relationships of mutual
service within the community of those whose lives are being
transformed by the Spirit in conformity to the character of
Christ'.[9] While that definition may work in Galatians, I am not so
sure it works in 1 Corinthians. In 1 Corinthians 9:21, 'Christ's law'
stands in contrast to the other 'law', which is certainly the law of
Moses, the Torah. Paul's logic seems to be that sometimes, for the
sake of the mission to the Gentiles, he lives as one outside the
Mosaic law.

But that does not mean he is lawless, because he remains bound
to God's law by being under the law of Christ. This cannot be that
God has one set of laws for Jews and another set of laws for
Gentiles, because (1) Paul is a Jew and can happily live under either
law if need be, and (2) the law of Christ is not necessarily opposed
in content to the law of Moses, even if they are not the same thing.
I am inclined to see the 'law of Christ' as signifying the full range
of commands and exhortations that belong to the messianic age
inaugurated by Christ, which would include the example of Christ,
the teaching of Christ and the law of love. In other words, the 'law
of Christ' is a synecdoche or emblematic catchword referring to
the whole substance of Christian moral teaching.

Life in the Spirit
Paul often places the law and Spirit in binary opposition to one
another: 'But if you are led by the Spirit, you are not under the law'
(Gal. 5:18) and 'For the letter kills, but the Spirit gives life' (2 Cor.

---

9. B. Longenecker, *The Triumph of Abraham's God* (Edinburgh: T. & T. Clark,
    1998), p. 86.

3:6). Even though Christians are under grace, not law, it does not legitimize a lawless lifestyle. Life in the Spirit is a life of righteousness and holiness. The Holy Spirit is the Spirit of Holiness. Since Christians are led by the Spirit, they must put off the works of the flesh, and instead cultivate the 'fruit of the Spirit', which includes 'love, joy, peace, patience, kindness, goodness, faithfulness, gentleness and self-control'. Paul goes on to say, 'And those who belong to Christ Jesus have crucified the flesh with its passions and desires. If we live by the Spirit, let us also walk by the Spirit' (Gal. 5:22–25).

A similar pattern occurs in Romans 8, 'For the law of the Spirit of life in Christ Jesus has set you free from the law of sin and death' (Rom. 8:2), with the result that 'the righteous requirement of the law might be fulfilled in us, who walk not according to the flesh but according to the Spirit' (Rom. 8:4). Paul sets Spirit in opposition to law, but also sets it in opposition to the 'flesh', warning in very strong terms that those who live by the flesh will die and not enter the eternal kingdom (Rom. 8:6, 13; Gal. 5:21; 1 Cor. 6:9–10; 15:50). A life in the 'flesh' is singularly *inappropriate* for believers, because 'you were washed, you were sanctified, you were justified in the name of the Lord Jesus Christ and by the Spirit of our God' (1 Cor. 6:11). F. F. Bruce writes, 'The Spirit is the sanctifying agency in the lives of believers: he wages perpetual warfare against the flesh, but he is more powerful than the flesh, and can put the flesh progressively out of action in those lives which are yielded to his control.'[10]

The law of love

Love was not a concept foreign to the law or to Jews in the first century. Love for God (Deut. 6:5) and love for neighbours (Lev. 19:18) was at the heart of the law and Judaism. Jesus wonderfully combined these two themes when asked about what was the greatest commandment (Mark 12:29–31). At a time when divisive debates were erupting in various churches, while believers were

---

10. F. F. Bruce, *Paul: Apostle of the Free Spirit*, rev. ed. (Carlisle, UK: Paternoster, 1980), p. 210.

given over to selfish ambition and were seeking their own good and honour, Paul argued for the supremacy of love in their relations with one another. The centrality of love in Paul's ethics is more than evident:

> Let love be sincere, hate what is evil, hold fast to what is good, love one another with mutual devotion, esteem the honour of others.
>   (Rom. 12:9–10)

> Owe no one anything, except to love one another; for the one loving another has fulfilled the law.
>   (Rom. 13:8)

> If your brother or sister is being wounded by what you eat, you are no longer walking in love. Do not let food destroy the one for whom Christ died.
>   (Rom. 14:15)

> Now concerning food sacrificed to idols: we know that 'all of us possess knowledge'. Knowledge puffs up, but love builds up.
>   (1 Cor. 8:1)

> Let all that you do be done in love.
>   (1 Cor. 16:14)

> For in Christ Jesus neither circumcision nor uncircumcision has any value; but all that counts is faith working through love.
>   (Gal. 5:6)

> But the aim of such instruction is love.[11]
>   (1 Tim. 1:5)

For Paul, love means seeking the good of the other rather than the good of oneself. The love command is indeed the fulfilment of

---

11. See also 1 Cor. 13:1–13; 14:1; Gal. 5:13–14; Eph. 4:15–16; 5:2; 6:23; Phil. 1:9; 2:1–2; Col. 3:14; 1 Thess. 3:12; 4:9; 5:8; 1 Tim. 1:5; 4:12.

the law itself (Gal. 5:14; Rom. 13:9). Paul's timeless and beautiful reflections about love in 1 Corinthians 13:1–13 are not an interruption in the text of 1 Corinthians as if Paul suddenly remembered, halfway through refereeing a debate about worship and spiritual gifts in Corinth, to write something that would give Christians for all generations a text to read at weddings. The debate in 1 Corinthians 12 – 14 is about what constitutes true worship and the mark of being truly spiritual. Paul's moving meditation on love shows that true worship and real spirituality are measured in love, not in pyrotechnic displays of spiritual power that draw attention to oneself.

And what of the Mosaic law in Christian ethics?

If these four points are the building blocks of Paul's ethics, then what about the Decalogue or Ten Commandments? Surely the Ten Commandments feature prominently in the life of the Christian according to Paul? To put it bluntly, not necessarily! In the Reformed tradition, it has been common to divide the law into three parts, *civil*, *ceremonial* and *moral*, and then to suggest that Christ fulfilled the civil and ceremonial law, but the moral law (as defined by the Ten Commandments) endures and continues into the new-covenant era. The problem here is twofold.

First, Jews in antiquity did not divide the law neatly into three parts of civil, ceremonial and moral. For them, Torah was Torah, *nomos* (Greek for 'law') was *nomos*, an indissoluble unity, all of which had to be obeyed since it was all commanded by God. The Jews of antiquity did not pick and choose which parts of the Mosaic law they thought were relevant to their predicament. Apart from the problem of what constitutes 'moral law' (the Sabbath could be described as both moral and ceremonial on some definitions), the division of the law imposes a foreign categorization onto how Jews like Paul read their Scriptures. In fact, the earliest document to separate the Mosaic law into three parts was a later Gnostic writing called the *Gospel of Truth*, which divides the law into commandments given by God, Moses and the elders of the people (*Gos. Truth* 19–21).

Second, moral law is found outside the Decalogue in the Torah, and pertains to sexuality, communal justice and state governance. While the Decalogue certainly sums up the moral teaching of the Torah, it does not exhaust it. Thus, it is anachronistic to divide the law into three parts and arbitrary to focus on the Decalogue as the exclusive moral component of the law.

However, that is not to say that Paul found no occasion to affirm a place for the Mosaic law in his ethical exhortations. On the relationship of the law to life in the new creation, Paul declares that 'circumcision and uncircumcision count for nothing'; instead, what counts is 'keeping the commandments of God' (1 Cor. 7:19). This means that while the new creation relativizes the distinctions made within the law by placing them in a new eschatological framework, it does not mean the obliteration of any sense of moral order from the law that continues into God's new creative act. Additionally, in Romans, Paul says, 'The commandments, "You shall not commit adultery, You shall not kill, You shall not steal, You shall not covet," and any other commandment, are summed up in this word, "You shall love your neighbour as yourself"' (Rom. 13:9). The love command was a frequent way of summarizing the law according to Christian (Matt. 5:43–48; 19:19; 22:34–40; Gal. 5:14; Jas 2:8) and Jewish (*b. Šabb.* 31a; *Sifra* 19.18) traditions. The love command is the summary, epitome and condensation of the entire law, and is not opposed to it.[12] While love fulfils the law, doing the law is an expression of love, or, put differently, treating others along the lines of the Decalogue is one of the most loving things someone can do.

Convictions and commands

The early church was characterized by a great deal of diversity. Alas, not everyone was a redhead Reformed Baptist with an Australian accent and a Pauline view of the law.[13] This diversity

---

12. Dunn, *Theology of Paul the Apostle*, p. 656.

13. Some scholars here would ask, 'Which Pauline view of the law? His view from earlier in his apostolic career, or his mature and developed view of

was apparent more than anywhere else in the wide-ranging views about the continuing relevance and function of the Jewish law in Christian communities. Consider the following examples that summarize positions on the law taken from the New Testament:[14]

- Jewish Christians and Gentile converts who insisted on full observance of the Mosaic law, including circumcision.
- Jewish Christians and Gentile converts who did not insist on circumcision, but did require converts to keep some Jewish observances.
- Jewish Christians and Gentile converts who did not insist on circumcision or adherence to the Jewish food laws.
- Jewish Christians and Gentile converts who did not insist on circumcision, adherence to the Jewish food laws or Jewish cults and feasts.

Everyone agreed that the coming of the Messiah had brought a change to the current state of things, and even the ancient law of Israel was affected by this. The questions that remained were, 'Who has to observe the law, which laws, why and under what circumstances?' Even if one argues that Jewish Christians have to

---

Footnote 13 (*continued*)

the law taken from later in his career? The view of the law found in Galatians or that contained in Romans? Paul's view of the law in his letters, or Paul's view of the law as depicted in the Acts of the Apostles?' While there is a great deal of complexity to the subject of Paul and the law, I would be prepared to argue that, despite the prospect of gradual and maturing developments in Paul's thinking on this subject, given the diverse situations and contexts he faced, and in the light of Paul's reactionary responses and his largely unsystematic thoughts on the subject, there was still a coherent line of thought traceable throughout his letters. This line of thought demonstrates that Christ and Torah are antitheses when it comes to the impotence of the law to effect salvation and it denies the law a role in formulating the boundaries of the people of God.

14. Gleaned from R. Brown and J. Meier, *Antioch and Rome: New Testament Cradles of Catholic Christianity* (New York: Paulist, 1983), pp. 1–9.

observe the law, but Gentile Christians do not have to, what happens when you have a mixed congregation with Jews and Gentiles sharing fellowship at the dinner table (see Gal. 2:11–14)? Do Jewish Christians give up their food laws to accommodate Gentiles, or do the Gentiles accede to the scruples of their Jewish brothers and sisters? Is it pork sandwiches for everyone, or mutton–lettuce–tomato on rye?

We should note that while Paul defended the right of Gentiles to be free from the forcible imposition of the law upon them, he did not demand that Jewish Christians give up all observance of the law.[15] Although this is not the place to enter into lengthy debates about the Torah in early Christianity,[16] I want to show just how Paul's instruction for mixed congregations with competing convictions over the Mosaic law furnishes an excellent example of

---

15. It is important to note that even with Paul's critique of the law and his vehement efforts to repel its imposition upon Gentiles, he did not have a problem with Jewish Christians desiring or choosing to follow the law. W. S. Campbell writes, 'Because Paul cannot yield on this point [the gospel is available to Gentiles without having to proselytize] does not mean that he opposed all things Jewish or that he would discourage Jewish Christians from following a Jewish lifestyle after they had become Christians. This stipulation that Jewish Christians recognise the right of Gentile Christians to be accepted into the people of God and continue to live a Gentile (Christian) lifestyle, does not mean that such Jewish Christians as recognised this should not also have the freedom to continue to live in a Jewish lifestyle. New Testament scholars have in the past tended to presume that all Jewish Christians who wished to continue to follow a Jewish lifestyle must necessarily deny the right of Gentile Christians to follow a Gentile lifestyle. But logic does not demand this conclusion. The two positions i.e. Jewish Christians continuing to follow a Jewish pattern of life, and Gentile Christians continuing to follow a Gentile pattern of life, are not mutually exclusive' (*Paul's Gospel in an Intercultural Context: Jew and Gentile in the Letter to the Romans* [Frankfurt am Main: Peter Lang, 1992], p. 100).

16. See the stimulating work by M. Bockmuehl, *Jewish Law in Gentile Churches: Halakhah and the Beginning of Christian Public Ethics* (Edinburgh: T. & T. Clark, 2000).

the way Christians with differing opinions on secondary matters can live and worship together in God-honouring harmony.

Pursue the things that make for peace

The most contentious debates in the early church were not over the ordination of women, nor worship music, nor whether to baptize infants; rather, they were about *food and fellowship*.

In 1 Corinthians 8, Paul deals with the subject of whether Christians should eat food offered to idols. In cities like Corinth, most of the meat sold in the marketplace was the leftover from banquets held in pagan temples, where the meat had been dedicated to a pagan deity before consumption. Evidently some Christians had very strong feelings that it was wrong to eat this meat because of its associations with their former pagan way of life or due to biblical injunctions against idolatry (1 Cor. 8:7). Paul's response is that we know that an idol has no real existence and meat is just meat, so do not worry about what you eat. However, if you are in the company of a fellow believer who has strong feelings about such things and is easily offended about eating meat offered to idols, then the responsibility of the Christian is not to eat such meat, 'lest I should make my brother stumble' (1 Cor. 8:13).

In Romans 14:1 – 15:7, Paul makes similar remarks. The issues in Romans are vegetarianism, wine and the observance of Jewish holy days. Paul is mediating between a group whom he labels the 'weak' and another he calls the 'strong'. But who were they? It is probable that the 'weak' were Jewish Christians and the 'strong', Gentile Christians, although we should not overlook the possibility that some Jewish Christians like Paul considered themselves to be among the 'strong', and Gentile Christians who formerly observed Jewish customs as God-fearers or proselytes could quite easily constitute the 'weak'. Importantly, 'weak' here does not mean 'weak in faith'; it means, rather, possessing a conscience more easily transgressed. In the Greco-Roman world, weakness could designate 'an intense belief in which someone regards a thing that needs not be shunned as though it ought to be shunned' (Cicero, *Tusc.* 4.22). Avoiding all meat could relate either to asceticism or to a desire to avoid the impurity associated with Gentile food (e.g. Dan. 1:8–16).

Paul's primary concern is that the 'strong' do not deliberately offend the 'weak' by their actions and that the 'strong' do not allow themselves to be bullied by the 'weak' in their accommodation of them. To that end, Paul argues as follows:

1. Leave judgment on disputable matters to God, for you cannot condemn the one whom God has justified.
2. Do not make food a stumbling block to others, since the kingdom of God is not a matter of eating and drinking but of righteousness and peace and joy in the Holy Spirit.
3. Do not reject someone who serves Christ and is therefore acceptable to God.
4. Those who eat or abstain, whether strong or weak, do so as an act of faith towards God.
5. There is a mutual obligation upon each person to accept one another and to build each other up in the faith.

Note that Paul does not argue for an uniform view of meat, drink and Sabbath observances, but recognizes the freedom of individuals to decide such matters for themselves. This is born out of the conviction that what unites Christians is infinitely stronger than anything that might tear them apart. My favourite verse from Romans (and one I wish were read before all church meetings) is this: 'Let us then pursue the things that make for peace and for mutual upbuilding' (Rom. 14:19). While you will not find food sacrificed to idols at Tesco or Wal-Mart, consider the plight of Christians in Asia and the struggle they face with their Buddhist families as to whether or not they should eat food that has been offered to their ancestors. What Paul says here is just as applicable to disputable matters about whether or not Christians should drink alcohol or about what television shows Christians should or should not watch.

Putting Paul's teachings into practice
In terms of application, 1 Corinthians 8 and Romans 14:1 – 15:7 have the following relevance:

- Learn to differentiate between areas of conviction and areas of command.
- Don't major on minor doctrines.
- Withhold judgment where the gospel is not threatened.
- Exercise your convictions to build others up, not to tear them down.
- Do not exchange freedom in Christ for slavery to human tradition.
- At all times act in love and fulfil the law of Christ.

Freedom, liberty and licence

Paul is undoubtedly the 'Apostle of Liberty',[17] but that liberty is not without limits. On the one hand, Paul can say, 'For the law of the Spirit of life in Christ Jesus has set you free from the law of sin and of death' (Rom. 8:2), and 'For freedom Christ has set us free' (Gal. 5:1). On the other hand, he warns against misuse of freedom for the purpose of cultivating sin: 'But do not use your freedom to indulge the sinful nature' (Gal. 5:13; see 1 Cor. 6:12; 10:23). There is a continuum between the extremes of licence and legalism, which are balanced by the conviction of liberty and by the imperative of love.[18]

```
                             LIBERTY

LICENCE ─────────────────────────────────────── LEGALISM
              LOVE                    LOVE
```

Achieving this balance as a person, family, church or denomination can be hard. But in many ways it comes down to a matter of whom we choose to honour. Christians should honour God with their bodies (1 Cor. 6:19–20) and show zeal in trying to honour one another above themselves (Rom. 12:10).

---

17. Cf. R. N. Longenecker, *Paul, Apostle of Liberty* (New York: Harper & Row, 1964).

18. Dunn, *Theology of Paul the Apostle*, p. 660.

Paul, sex and women

Paul is not anywhere as interested in sex as many of his recent commentators are. For the most part, the Christian tradition, following Paul, has advocated celibacy in singleness and faithfulness in marriage as the norm for Christians. Much of this is indebted to the Old Testament (Lev. 18 − 20), which prohibits adultery, incest, bestiality and homosexuality. Paul urges Christians to abstain from joining themselves to prostitutes (1 Cor. 6:15−16), from adultery (Rom. 13:9; 1 Cor. 6:9; 1 Tim. 1:10), sexual immorality (Rom. 1:24; 13:13; 1 Cor. 5:1; 6:13; 7:2; 10:8; 2 Cor. 12:21; Gal. 5:19; Eph. 5:3; Col. 3:5; 1 Thess. 4:3) and homosexuality (Rom. 1:26−28; 1 Cor. 6.9; 1 Tim. 1:10). Paul's most concise treatment of sex is of course found in 1 Corinthians 7. There he advocates the value of singleness but has no problem with marriage, for he wants married couples to enjoy healthy sexual relations. He knows that divorce is prohibited by Jesus, but understands that divorce sometimes happens.

Ultimately, Paul's view is that sex and sexuality are God's gift to humans, but with the various prohibitions about sex one might think Paul thought it very important to restrict Christians from enjoying sexual relations too much. Nothing could be further from the truth. All of the prohibitions are quite practical as well. In our culture, pre-marital sex might seem the norm given the widespread availability of contraception and abortion, and even if the contraception does not work, we have a welfare system to help single parents − but not so in the ancient world. What is more, intimacy without commitment is not healthy for any relationship. Pornography degrades women and the relationship men have with women. Adultery is the most painful act of betrayal one can perform in a relationship. Sexual immorality in general can force a person to become addicted or controlled by the sexual impulse. A sex-obsessed culture leaves women and especially children vulnerable to being overly sexualized and exploited.

What makes these things a sin is not that God is the cosmic killjoy; rather, they represent a rejection of God's intention for human sexuality. These acts also have painful effects in the web of human relationships and result in unhealthy outcomes for society in general. A society that has rejected God will be driven to pursue power or pleasure, the fist or the phallus, Hitler or Heffner. That is not how the story is supposed to go. The good news is that Paul can also say that everyone is invited to church: adulterers, homosexuals, whoremongers, sex-addicts and sexual deviants of every kind. You may come as you are, but no one is allowed to stay that way. For all have sinned and fall short of the glory of God and need to hear the good news of redemption and experience the transforming power of the Spirit to enable men and women to become the renewed humanity he always intended them to be (see Rom. 3:21–26; Col. 3:1–17).

Now let us take a closer look at Paul and homosexuality, a topic that requires attention to detail and pastoral sensitivity. The Old Testament at several points explicitly forbids homosexual acts (e.g. Lev. 18:22; 20:13), and this finds thematic repetition at several places in Paul's letters (Rom. 1:26–27; 1 Cor. 6:9–10; 1 Tim. 1:10). Paul's statements must be placed in their cultural context, where homosexuality, as both a sexual act and a relationship, was well known in the ancient world. For unmarried men in the Greco-Roman world the primary means of sexual release were through slaves, raping during war, prostitutes or with same-sex partners. Gay marriages were not unknown either, since Nero had two gay marriages involving his slaves. In one marriage he was the groom (he married his slave Sporus, whom he first had castrated) and in another marriage (to Phytagoras) he was the bride. Women having sexual relations with other women was a frequent occurrence, which even became a matter of concern to male authors in the late republican and early imperial Roman periods.[19]

For some authors, homosexuality, in moderation, was simply part of life and one of the highest expressions of love (e.g. Plato, *Symp.* 178C–180B). Alternatively, some Greco-Roman authors could argue that it was 'contrary to nature' (Plato, *Laws* 1.2), or else they could reject any man being the effeminate or dominated partner in a relationship (Julius Caesar incurred disgust from his troops because he was rumoured to have allowed himself to have

---

19. C. H. Talbert, *Romans* (Macon: Smyth & Helwys, 2002), p. 65.

been the submissive partner in a relationship with Nicomedes, the king of Bithynia). For the most part, it was the unnatural character of homosexuality that constituted the Jewish objection to it as a sinful practice. For instance, the Egyptian Jewish philosopher Philo wrote, 'They discard the laws of nature . . . for not only did they go mad after women, and defile the marriage bed of others, but also those who were men lusted after one another' (*Abr.* 135). This is the context of Paul's comments in Romans:

> For this reason God gave them up to dishonourable passions. Their women exchanged natural relations for unnatural relations, and the men likewise gave up the natural use of women and were inflamed with passion for one another, men in men committing shameless acts and receiving in their own persons the necessary penalty for their error.
> (Rom. 1:26–27)

We can make several observations about Paul's remarks here: (1) He is talking about the homosexual activity of both men and women; (2) rejection of the created design for human sexuality is symptomatic of rejection of the Creator; (3) sexual acts of this order dishonour both God and human beings; and (4) the consequences of homosexual practices (physical, emotional, psychological) in a sense constitute their own punishment.

These homosexual practices are part of the web of sin and rebellion that prompts God to reveal his wrath against humankind. Of course, several alternative readings are often put forward, such as that Paul is condemning only pederasty,[20] or heterosexuals engaged in homosexual promiscuity, sexual exploitation of slaves, or homosexuality in the context of pagan worship. Such interpretations can persist only by doing serious violence to the context and content of Paul's argument. Paul's proscriptions are broad enough to apply to an assortment of homosexual relations and acts (including those of men and women) and his argument in

---

20. Pederasty is homosexual relations between an adult and an adolescent. It is possible that this is what is in mind in 1 Cor. 6:9, but even there Paul condemns both the active (*arsenokoitēs*) and effeminate (*malakos*) partners.

Romans 1 encompasses the unnatural nature of homosexuality itself.

Many commentators argue that Paul's remarks about homosexuality have to be qualified in that Paul did not know of sexual orientation or of long-term same-sex relationships. Yet it is nonsense to say that Paul did not know of committed same-sex relationships, for they were quite common. There were those who argued that homosexuality was an entirely natural occurrence (Philostratus, *Ep.* 64; Aristotle, *Eth. nic.* 7.5.3–5) and a philosophically superior type of love (Callicratidas in Pseudo-Lucian, *Affairs of the Heart*).[21] Paul's view, and that of subsequent Christian thought, is that homosexuality is not what humans were created for and has a dehumanizing effect on those engaged in such acts. Though I wish to add that for Paul, homosexual sins are not any worse or any viler than heterosexual sins: God does not have a special loathing reserved for gays and lesbians. While Christians, as a response to homosexuality, toss around pithy one-liners like 'welcoming but not affirming' or 'hate the sin but love the sinner', probably the best response is what Paul himself says in Romans 13:9 when he quotes Leviticus 19:18, 'Love your neighbour as yourself' (see also Matt. 19:19; 22:39; Mark 12:33; Luke 10:27).[22]

When it comes to women, Paul has been a source of great controversy. Several texts speak of the authority of the husband over the wife (1 Cor. 11:2–16; Eph. 5:22–33; Col. 3:18). In 1 Timothy 2:11–15, Paul restricts the role of women in teaching men at Ephesus, probably due to the advent of a heresy that was attempting to redefine the role of women by distorting the creation narrative. For our consideration there are clear indications in the New Testament that women on some occasions had a teaching ministry in the Pauline churches. Priscilla and Aquila both taught Apollos (Acts 18:26), female prophets prophesied in Christian

21. See further R. J. Gagnon, *The Bible and Homosexual Practice: Texts and Hermeneutics* (Nashville: Abingdon, 2001), which is without peer as a book about what the Bible has to say about homosexuality.

22. I owe this point to my friend Scot McKnight, who says this on his website, <http://www.jesuscreed.org>.

gatherings (Acts 21:9; 1 Cor. 11:5), in the early church there were women who were the heads of households and they potentially exercised some form of leadership in house churches (1 Cor. 1:11; Acts 16:14–15; Col. 4:15). Also Euodia, Syntyche and Priscilla are called Paul's 'co-workers' (*synergos*) in the gospel (Phil. 4:3; Rom. 16:3); the same word is used elsewhere to describe the ministry of prominent Christian leaders in the Pauline circle (e.g. Rom. 16:9, 21; 1 Cor. 16:15–16; 2 Cor. 8:23; Phil. 2:25; Col. 4:11; 1 Thess. 3:2; Phlm. 1, 24). Even a female apostle, Junia, is mentioned at the end of Romans (Rom. 16:7).[23] A certain Phoebe, whom Paul trusted to deliver his letter to Rome, is called a 'servant' of the church in Cenchreae (Rom. 16:1).

While Paul for the most part shared the patriarchal perspective of the ancient world, he also speaks of mutual submission (Eph. 5:21) and a mutual authority (1 Cor. 7:4) between husbands and wives. In a passage shocking to the cultural sensibilities of the time, Paul states that 'There is neither Jew nor Greek, there is neither slave nor free, there is neither *male and female* – for all of you are one in Christ Jesus' (Gal. 3:28). This verse is often quoted out of context and misused. Paul is not saying that for Christians gender ceases to exist as if God has decided henceforth only to look at people from the neck up, thus proving the irrelevance of gender. Neither is Paul stating that this unity only applies to equality in salvation, thus proving that Christians should maintain patriarchal practices. What he is saying is that the glory of the new creation made known in Christ means the negation of the distinctions that have ordinarily separated human beings from one another. Neither race, nor class, nor gender places one closer to the throne of God. The family of Abraham is a diverse family

---

23. Based on textual evidence from manuscripts about Romans 16:7, in his magisterial study Eldon Epp has recently concluded that the extant witnesses treat Junia as an apostle. He concludes, 'It remains a fact that there was a woman apostle, explicitly so named, in the earliest generation of Christianity, and contemporary Christians – lay people and clergy – must (and eventually will) face up to it' (Eldon J. Epp, *Junia: The First Woman Apostle* [Minneapolis: Fortress, 2005], p. 81).

with children from every nation, rich and poor, male and female. This underscores the equality principle of the gospel, where all persons stand before God on the same level and no one has the inside track or can plead they are better or more useful than any other person.

Conclusion

In Paul's view, one's intellectual and practical lives are necessarily intertwined. There is no room to accommodate a dry cerebral faith that does not issue forth in action; nor is there a place for a Christian lifestyle that is not at once rooted in theological reflection of the gospel. What will ultimately separate the sheep from the goats at the final assize will not be a theology exam, but whether our walk matched our words, and whether we have deeds born out of faith. While we are not saved by works, we shall not be saved without them. Justification at the final day will exclusively be due to the work of Christ, but the same Christ works his works in us, and these works demonstrate the integrity of our faith. As the Danish philosopher Søren Kierkegaard is reported to have said, *as you have lived so have you believed*. What ultimately defines one's true beliefs is not words or pithy slogans, but a life lived before God among other human beings. Paul, therefore, urges the churches with severe warnings and warm encouragements to live a life worthy of the gospel and to render loyal and faithful service to their Lord. Tom Schreiner gives a neat summary of Paul's ethics:

> Believers are enabled to live a new life by virtue of the work of Christ on their behalf and through the power of the indwelling Holy Spirit. God's work, however, does not cancel out the response to human beings but establishes it. The indicative is the basis for the imperative, and Paul summons his churches to live out the gospel they have embraced.[24]

---

24. Schreiner, *Paul*, p. 270.

10. GOSPELIZING 101: PAUL'S SPIRITUALITY

For Paul, Christian life is the gospel-driven life. The centrality of the gospel is evident from the very grammar of Paul's letters that points to the gospel as being integral to Christian faith and life. We can speak of God and pray to God only as he is known as the 'God of the gospel' (Rom. 1:1; 15:16; 2 Cor. 11:7; 1 Thess. 2:8–9). I cannot refrain from quoting John Webster, who states, 'The matter to which Christian theology is commanded to attend, and by which it is directed in all its operations, is the presence of the perfect God as it is announced in the gospel.'[1] According to Paul, Christology is understanding the 'man Christ Jesus' (1 Tim. 2:5) and the 'gospel of Christ' (Rom. 15:19; 1 Cor. 9:12; 2 Cor. 2:12; 9:13; 10:14; Gal. 1:7; Phil. 1:27; 1 Thess. 3:2).

Christian ethics means living a life 'worthy of the gospel' (Phil. 1:27) and exercising obedience that accompanies 'confession of

---

1. J. Webster, *Confessing God: Essays in Christian Dogmatics II* (London: T. & T. Clark, 2005), p. 1.

the gospel' (2 Cor. 9:13). The gift of the Spirit brings new birth
as part of the promise of the gospel (Rom. 5:5). Understanding
salvation in Christ means to unpack the polyphonic richness of
the gospel of salvation (Rom. 1:16; Eph. 1:13). Apologetics is
the 'defence of the gospel' (Phil. 1:16). Ecclesiology is the doctrine of the community of the gospelized, while missiology is
the science of gospelizing. Quite clearly, then, the chief contribu-
tor to this theology of the gospel in the New Testament is Paul.
The centre of Paul's theology, in so far as it is reflected in his
letters, is the good news of salvation in Christ Jesus.

The place of the gospel in theology and ministry is no mere
academic exercise but has real outcomes in terms of Christian life
and ministry. The process of discipleship is largely the process of
gospelization, that is, beginning to reflect in one's life the realities the
gospel endeavours to create (see chapter 9 above). Discipleship is
the process of 'gospelizing' ourselves so that both we and others
attain the full measure of maturity in Christ and walk in the foot-
steps of Christ in our own lives. We might say that with Paul this
gospelization works itself out in two major ways in the life of the
Christian: through being 'cruciformed' and 'anastasized'.

Cruciformity

Cruciformity: *to be shaped in accord with the cross of Christ.*[2]

> When I came to you, brothers and sisters, I did not come with superior
> eloquence or wisdom as I proclaimed the testimony of God. For I
> decided to be concerned about nothing among you except Jesus Christ,
> and him crucified.
>
> (1 Cor. 2:1–2, NET)

Imagine you are walking through your local university or college
and hear in the quad an elderly man from South America telling

---

2. M. J. Gorman, *Apostle of the Crucified Lord: A Theological Introduction to Paul
and His Letters* (Grand Rapids: Eerdmans, 2004), pp. 115–130.

people loudly about God's love and salvation. He announces the 'good news' of Carlos Hernandez. He recounts how Carlos was a Peruvian peasant attested by many mighty deeds of power and miracles and who proclaimed the end of the world. But the chief men in the city of Lima feared his popularity with the peasant class, falsely accused him of being an Al-Qaeda terrorist and had him killed by electrocution. But a week later, this Carlos was raised from the dead and was seen by several American tourists. Then the man declares that 'this Carlos was electrocuted for your sins and salvation is found through faith in him'. And then, to make matters worse, he starts singing:

> Carlos was there on that horrible chair
> They tied him down with bolts and then zapped him with 40,000 volts
> It was for you our saviour fried and died
> Despite the fact that his hair caught on fire, this one is God's true Messiah.
> The wisdom of the world has been refuted because Carlos was electrocuted
> He is my saviour and my lamp, because he absorbed every deadly amp
> Now I know that God does care, 'cause he sent Carlos Hernandez to the electric chair.

I do not want to push the analogy too far, but for Paul to proclaim in the cities of Athens, Thessalonica or Corinth that a Jew crucified by the Roman authorities was 'Saviour' and 'Lord' would probably have sounded very similar to how the report about Carlos Hernandez would sound to us. We would think it utter foolishness. That is exactly the attitude Paul encountered. The message of Christ crucified was foolishness to Greeks and a stumbling block to Jews (1 Cor. 1:18, 22–23; Rom. 9:32). The message of the cross divides human beings into two camps: those who are perishing and those who are being saved (1 Cor. 1:18). Through the cross, God exposes the wisdom of the world as a sham (1 Cor. 1:19–21). For those with the eyes of faith the cross is the embodiment of God's wisdom and power and Jesus is the source of wisdom, righteousness, holiness and redemption (1 Cor. 1:24–25, 30).

Furthermore, the Christian community itself is emblematic of that unexpected revelation of divine mercy, since God chose them despite their (for the most part) being neither powerful nor privileged. God chose the foolish and the weak, those who are invisible and expendable to society, and made them vessels that reveal his power and wisdom (1 Cor. 1:26–29). God's seeming foolishness in the cross is matched only by the seeming foolishness of his choice of those whom he called to be recipients of salvation. The weakness, the inferiority and the mediocrity of those whom God has called for salvation is a living metaphor of the cross: God reveals his salvation where it is least expected.

The important thing is that the cross is not only the means of salvation, but the pattern of life and example we are called to follow. Christians are called to believe a foolish message and live a foolish lifestyle. The cross must shape our spirituality, attitudes, values and ministry, what we fear, flee from and try to be as Christians and as churches. This carries with it several corollaries.

First, a community that ceases to be a living metaphor of the cross has exchanged God's wisdom for human foolishness. That was the problem in Corinth. Many of the Corinthians were mesmerized by displays of spiritual power and wanted a Christ without a cross to feed their preoccupation with status, power, wisdom and influence.

Second, a community that embodies the cross will reflect the character of God in mutual forgiveness (2 Cor. 2:7, 10). In Colossians, forgiveness between Christians is a means to communal peace: 'Bear with one another and, if anyone has a complaint against another, forgive each other; just as the Lord has forgiven you, so you also must forgive' (Col. 3:13). Forgiveness flows from the Lord to them and to others in their rank, as a necessity, a command, and not as an option.

Third, a community shaped by the cross will overflow with love. For Paul the true test of spirituality is not in any display of spiritual pyrotechnics but in love (1 Cor. 13:1–13). Christians are to 'pursue love' (1 Cor. 14:1), and whatever they do, it 'must be done in love' (1 Cor. 16:14).

Fourth, a cruciform community follows the pattern of Christ's example. Paul asks the Corinthians to imitate him only in so far as

he imitates Christ (1 Cor. 11:1). That is why Paul can urge
Christians to 'put on Christ' as if they were putting on a new
garment (Rom. 13:14; Gal. 3:27). Believers are to discard the old
way of life, put on the pattern of new life and cultivate the values
and attitudes that go with being a new creation. This is not take-it-
or-leave-it advice; it is the constitution for a new society and the
code of conduct for a new citizenry. In the sublime Christ hymn
of Philippians 2:5–11 we looked at earlier, the predominant image
is that of Christ being a servant. Consequently, Christ's followers
are to become servants to one another. We should all remember
that the greatest test of whether or not we have a servant's heart is
how we act when we are treated like a servant.

Fifth, a community of faith that clings to the cross will consist-
ently find itself at odds with the world. Paul can say that 'the world
has been crucified to me and I to it' (Gal. 6:14). In other words
Paul renounces all the world's values in favour of the values of the
cross. Discipleship will mean dying daily to what the world has to
offer, saying no to sin and yes to holiness, grasping Christ and
letting go of worldly trinkets, seeking the kingdom and not worldly
success.

Sixth, a community that takes up its cross will discover its identity in the cross. Paul states in Galatians, 'I have been crucified with
Christ, and it is no longer I who live, but Christ lives in me. So the
life I now live in the body, I live because of the faithfulness of the
Son of God, who loved me and gave himself for me' (Gal. 2:20,
NET). This means that the self-reference 'I' exists only with a line
through it, which turns the 'I' into a † (cross). I am known only as
one who has been crucified with Christ. Michael Bird is dead, co-
crucified with a Jewish martyr, and yet Bird lives on by some
strange and wonderful quickening in union with the crucified
Messiah and Lord who transfigures his personality, salvages his
soul and renews the inner bowels of his being. I am dead to the
world but alive in Jesus Christ. What inspires and sustains me is
not promises of power or the trappings of worldly success but the
inexhaustible love of Christ. I entrust myself to his faithfulness to
sustain me in the task to which he has appointed me.

Thus, the lesson from Paul is that a spirituality rooted in anything other than the cross of Christ will inevitably become novel,

then triumphalistic, then wishy-washy, then worldly, then trivial
and, finally, stone dead. For Paul Christian spirituality is not a
private matter that takes place in the mental events of our thought
life, but is manifested in action. A cruciform spirituality means not
merely wearing a cross but *carrying* one as well (Mark 8:34).

Anastasisity

Anastasisity: *to be made alive by the power of Christ's resurrection.*

> Therefore we have been buried with him through baptism into death, in
> order that just as Christ was raised from the dead through the glory of
> the Father, so we too may live a new life.
>   (Rom. 6:4, NET)

Evangelical theology, with its healthy fixation on the cross, has
often neglected the resurrection to the point that the resurrection
becomes little more than the proof of what God did on the cross.[3]
We have affirmed that the cross is central to Paul's gospel, but so is
the resurrection (e.g. 1 Cor. 15:17; Rom. 4:25). This neglect of the
resurrection extends not only to theology but also to spirituality.
But how does the resurrection impact our spiritual journey and
our Christian walk? The answer is, in several ways.

First, Paul says that believers 'have been made alive with Christ'
(Col. 2:12; 3:1; Eph. 2:6). This expression shows that in the here
and now, Christians already experience the life-giving power of
God in the vitalizing work of the Spirit. While their outer nature is
wasting away, their inner nature is being renewed (2 Cor. 4:16). For
the believer, the life of heaven is embryonically here on earth.

Second, the resurrection imparts hope to Christians. In an age
when most people ebb between the fear of death and the futility of
life (cf. Heb. 2:14–15), Paul can say that the brick of Christian hope
is the future resurrection of believers. That hope is as yet unseen,

3. Cf. M. F. Bird, *The Saving Righteousness of God: Studies in Paul, Justification, and
the New Perspective*, PBM (Milton Keynes: Paternoster, 2007), pp. 40–59.

so we wait with patience, until what is unseen becomes what is seen (Rom. 8:24–25). Christian hope is not a placebo in the face of certain death, but has substance and is confirmed by Christ's own resurrection as the prototype of what will happen to them.

Third, the resurrection is a motivation to press on towards the goal for which Christ has called believers. Paul states:

> I want to know Christ and the power of his resurrection and the fellowship of his sufferings by becoming like him in his death, if somehow I might attain the resurrection from the dead. Not that I have already obtained this or have already reached the goal; but I press on to make it my own, because Christ Jesus has made me his own.
>
> (Phil. 3:10–12)

The promise of resurrection provides Christians with hope in the face of fear, suffering and death. Hermann Ridderbos says this:

> Thus suffering, too, becomes a token of victory, because it leads one in the footprints of Christ. But this conjunction of death and life, of suffering and resurrection, is not only a pattern that is to be gathered from Christ's death and resurrection, a program that one could automatically follow; it is, with all the knowledge of Christ, a wrestling, a stretching out with every effort of the soul toward that which has not yet been attained.[4]

Christians are not on the wagon wheel of a thousand incarnations until they get it right, but are heading for a termination point where the life promised becomes the life given. I am no self-help guru, but I know that you are more likely to succeed in a race, in a struggle, in a task and in a mission if you start with a picture of the end in mind. You are more likely to finish a race if you can see the finishing line, know where the finishing line is or at least know that there is a finishing line.

---

4. H. Ridderbos, *Paul: An Outline of His Theology* (Grand Rapids: Eerdmans, 1975), p. 251. My thanks to Joshua Schow for bringing this quote to my attention.

Fourth, resurrection assures us of God's empowerment. The amazing thing about resurrection is that it attests the power of God's goodness and the goodness of God's power.[5] While a spirituality of the cross may make us think that unless we feel endlessly defeated, weak and miserable we are not living the Christian life properly, the resurrection brings a balance by showing us that God quickens and empowers those who live in weakness. Paul writes that Jesus 'was crucified in weakness, yet he lives by God's power. Likewise, we are weak in him, yet by God's power we shall live with him to serve you' (2 Cor. 13:4). God takes feeble, broken vessels, our weak selves, these cracked jars of clay, and infuses them with the divine enabling to accomplish his outrageous and awesome deeds through our acts of service. We live, serve and die by God's power, by God's grace and for God's glory.

---

5. L. E. Keck, *Who Is Jesus? History in Perfect Tense* (Columbia: University of South Carolina, 2000), p. 129.

11. EPILOGUE

It has been my aim in the preceding pages to lead readers on a brief exploration of Paul: his biography, his letters and the building blocks of his theology as revealed in his letters. However, we do not have the complete story on Paul by any stretch of the imagination. Instead, what we have through the letters is something like a clip of highlights from a film that played on the big screen long ago. We have not entered into the head of Paul and psychoanalysed him (as if that were possible), nor have we exhausted all there is to know about him. For such reasons we may come away with more questions than when we began. Yet that is precisely why Paul and his letters are so magnetic. Once you pick up Romans or 1 Corinthians or Philippians and start reading, things are never the same. Paul gets into your head and will never leave you be. There is no solving him, no domesticating him by way of any theological system, however elaborate, and there is no end to the maze of interpretations about him.

In wrestling with Paul, the joy is in the journey, not in reaching any destination of absolute comprehension about all he taught. That journey is, in Paul's own words, to 'press on toward the goal for the prize of the upward call of God in Christ Jesus' (Phil. 3:14). Unless we know Paul's Saviour, we do not really know Paul. Paul urges us to grow in knowledge and depth of insight about Christ so that we shall ultimately 'know him better' (Eph. 1:17). The goal of Paul's instruction is thus a closer relationship with the Lord Jesus Christ.

What of Paul's legacy, then? In the immediate historical sense, he fought for and won the right for Gentiles to join the church as Gentiles without having to become proselytes to Judaism, and so preserved the gospel from legalism and ethnocentrism. On top of that, theologically speaking, all great theologians (and notorious heretics) of history have taken their inspiration from Paul. From Origen to Karl Barth, renewal and reformation have followed from a fresh encounter with Paul. However, Paul's important legacy is that the Christian church, led by the witness of the Holy Spirit, has become convinced that what he wrote was Scripture. As Scripture his writings are divinely inspired and uniquely authoritative; that is to say, God spoke through Paul. To read Paul's letters, then, is to read the Word of God. This Word was not originally written *to* us, but it was written *for* us. Much like the Old Testament, Paul's letters were 'written to teach us, so that through endurance and the encouragement of the Scriptures we might have hope' (Rom. 15:4).

As to why Paul's letters are important for the church today, we can hardly fail to notice that for us in the West our pluralistic and postmodern world is becoming more and more like the ancient Greco-Roman world Paul lived in. There can be no question of our thinking of ourselves as chaplains for Christendom: those days are over. And if the church is to survive and flourish under such adverse circumstances, then we had better take heed to the things Paul taught.

In a world that is often cold, cruel, brutal and dark, Christians have a responsibility to shine like stars in setting up communities that radiate love and compassion. In a day when all claims to truth are suspected as being little more than veiled claims to power, Christians must set forth God's grace in all its truth. In an age when each man and woman does what seems right in his or her own eyes, where accountability is a byword, Christians must declare that every knee will bow to the Lord Jesus Christ, who is the appointed Judge of all angelic and human beings.

At a time when metanarratives, or claiming to possess an all-encompassing story of the universe, are denigrated as intolerant, Christians have to set forth the story of the gospel as the answer to the story of why the world has gone so horribly wrong. In a place of consumer spirituality and pocket guidebooks to heaven, Christians have to confront the world with the exclusive claims of the all-inclusive Saviour. In a culture where the greatest good is the gratification of the individual's hedonistic desires, Christians can set forth an alternative experience, where God offers an unspeakable joy that far outweighs the trappings and excesses of this world, which is fading away.

Above all, Paul reminds Christians today that we are walking billboards in the global metropolis, heralding the good news that God in Christ was reconciling the world to himself, and reminding onlookers that the day is coming when God will be all in all.

Finally, let us consider the Book of Common Prayer and the petition it has for us all in the light of the ministry of Paul:

> O God, who, through the preaching of the blessed Apostle Saint Paul, hast caused the light of the Gospel to shine throughout the world; Grant, we beseech thee, that we, having this wonderful conversion in remembrance, may shew forth our thankfulness unto thee for the same, by following the holy doctrine which he taught, through Jesus Christ our Lord. *Amen.*

BIBLIOGRAPHY

AULÉN, G., *Christus Victor: An Historical Study of the Three Main Types of the Idea of Atonement*, trans. A. G. Herber (New York: Macmillan, 1977).

AUNE, D. E., *The New Testament in its Literary Environment* (Cambridge: James Clark, 1987).

BAUCKHAM, R., *God Crucified: Monotheism and Christology in the New Testament* (Carlisle: Paternoster, 1998).

——, 'What if Paul Had Travelled East Rather Than West?', in *Virtual History and the Bible*, ed. J. C. Exum (Leiden: Brill, 1999), pp. 171–184.

BAUER, W., ARNDT, W. F., DANKER, F. W., and GINGRICH, W. F. (eds.), *A Greek–English Lexicon of the New Testament and other Early Christian Literature*, 3rd ed. (Chicago: University of Chicago Press, 2000).

BAUR, F. C., *Paul the Apostle of Jesus Christ: His Life and Works, His Epistles and Teachings: Two Volumes in One* (Peabody: Hendrickson, 2003 [1873–5]).

BEASLEY-MURRAY, P., 'Pastor, Paul as', in *DPL*, ed. G. F. Hawthorne, R. P. Martin and D. G. Reid (Downers Grove and Leicester: IVP, 1993), pp. 654–658.

BEKER, J. C., *Paul the Apostle: The Triumph of God in Life and Thought* (Philadelphia: Fortress, 1980).

BEST, E., *Paul and his Converts* (Edinburgh: T. & T. Clark, 1988).

BIRD, M. F., 'The Purpose and Preservation of the Jesus Tradition: Moderate Evidence for a Conserving Force in its Transmission', *BBR* 15 (2005), pp. 161–185.

——, *The Saving Righteousness of God: Studies in Paul, Justification, and the New Perspective*, PBM (Milton Keynes: Paternoster, 2007).

BLOMBERG, C. L., *From Pentecost to Patmos* (Nottingham: Apollos, 2006).

BOCKMUEHL, M., *Jewish Law in Gentile Churches: Halakhah and the Beginning of Christian Public Ethics* (Edinburgh: T. & T. Clark, 2000).

BROWN, R., and MEIER, J., *Antioch and Rome: New Testament Cradles of Catholic Christianity* (New York: Paulist, 1983).

BRUCE, F. F., *Paul: Apostle of the Free Spirit*, rev. ed. (Carlisle, UK: Paternoster, 1980).

BURKE, T. J., *Adopted into God's Family: Exploring a Pauline Metaphor* (Nottingham: Apollos; Downers Grove: IVP, 2006).

CAMPBELL, W. S., 'Israel', in *DPL*, ed. G. F. Hawthorne, R. P. Martin and D. G. Reid (Downers Grove and Leicester: IVP, 1993), pp. 441–446.

——, *Paul's Gospel in an Intercultural Context: Jew and Gentile in the Letter to the Romans* (Frankfurt am Main: Peter Lang, 1992).

CARSON, D. A., 'Atonement in Romans 3:21–26', in *The Glory of the Atonement. Biblical, Theological, and Practical Perspectives*, ed. C. E. Hill and F. A. James (Downers Grove: IVP; Leicester: Apollos, 2004), pp. 119–139.

CHARLESWORTH, J. H. (ed.), *The Old Testament Pseudepigrapha*, ABRL, 2 vols. (New York: Doubleday, 1983–5).

CRANFIELD, C. E. B., *The Epistle to the Romans*, ICC, 2 vols. (Edinburgh: T. & T. Clark, 1975–9).

CULLMANN, O., *Christ and Time*, trans. F. V. Filson (Philadelphia: Westminster, 1950).

DAHL, N. A., *Studies in Paul* (Minneapolis: Augsburg, 1977).

DESILVA, D. A., *4 Maccabees: Introduction and Commentary on the Greek Text of Codex Sinaiticus*, SCS (Leiden: Brill, 2006).

DUNN, J. D. G., *The Theology of Paul the Apostle* (Edinburgh: T. & T. Clark, 1998).

ELLIOTT, J. K. (ed.), *The Apocryphal New Testament: A Collection of Apocryphal Christian Literature in an English Translation Based on M. R. James* (Oxford: Clarendon, 1993).

EPP, E. J., *Junia: The First Woman Apostle* (Minneapolis: Fortress, 2005).

EVANS, C. A., *Mark 8:27–16:20*, WBC (Nashville: Thomas Nelson, 2001).

FEE, G. D., *Paul's Letter to the Philippians*, NICNT (Grand Rapids: Eerdmans, 1995).

FITZMYER, J. A., *Paul and His Theology: A Brief Sketch* (Englewood Cliffs: Prentice Hall, 1989).

GAGNON, R. J., *The Bible and Homosexual Practice: Texts and Hermeneutics* (Nashville: Abingdon, 2001).

GATHERCOLE, S., 'The Cross and Substitutionary Atonement', *SBET* 21

(2003), pp. 152–163.

GORDAY, P. (ed.), *Colossians, 1–2 Thessalonians, 1–2 Timothy, Titus, Philemon*, ACCS 9 (Downers Grove: IVP, 2000).

GORMAN, M. J., *Apostle of the Crucified Lord: A Theological Introduction to Paul and His Letters* (Grand Rapids: Eerdmans, 2004).

GREEN, J. B., and BAKER, M. D., *Recovering the Scandal of the Cross: Atonement in New Testament and Contemporary Contexts* (Carlisle, UK: Paternoster, 2000).

HARRISON, J. R., 'Paul and the Imperial Gospel at Thessaloniki', *JSNT* 25 (2002), pp. 71–96.

HAYS, R. B., *Echoes of Scripture in the Letters of Paul* (New Haven: Yale University Press, 1989).

——, *First Corinthians* (Louisville: Westminster John Knox, 1997).

HENGEL, M., *The Pre-Christian Paul*, trans. J. Bowden (London: SCM, 1991).

HOLLAND, T., *Contours of Pauline Theology* (Fearn, Ross-shire: Christian Focus, 2004).

HOLMES, S., 'Can Punishment Bring Peace? Penal Substitution Revisited', *SJT* 58 (2005), pp. 104–123.

HOOKER, M. D., *Jesus and the Servant* (London: SPCK, 1959).

——, 'Interchange in Christ', *JTS* 22 (1971), pp. 349–361.

HORACE, trans. J. Michie, *The Odes of Horace* (Harmondsworth: Penguin, 1964).

HULTGREN, A. J., *Paul's Gospel and Mission* (Philadelphia: Fortress, 1983).

JEFFERY, S., OVEY, M., and SACH, A., *Pierced for our Transgressions: Rediscovering the Glory of Penal Substitution* (Nottingham: IVP, 2007).

JERVIS, L. A., *At the Heart of the Gospel: Suffering in the Earliest Christian Message* (Grand Rapids: Eerdmans, 2007).

JONGE, M. DE, *God's Final Envoy: Early Christology and Jesus' Own View of His Mission* (Grand Rapids: Eerdmans, 1998).

JOSEPHUS, trans. W. Whiston, *The Complete Works of Josephus* (Peabody: Hendrickson, 1995).

KÄHLER, M., *Schriften zur Christologie und Mission* (Munich: C. Kaiser, 1971 [1908]).

KECK, LEANDER E., , 'Paul in New Testament Theology: Some Preliminary Remarks', in *The Nature of New Testament Theology*, ed. C. Rowland and C. Tuckett (Oxford: Blackwell, 2006), pp. 109–122.

——, *Romans*, ANTC (Nashville: Abingdon, 2005).

——, *Who Is Jesus? History in Perfect Tense* (Columbia: University of South

Carolina, 2000).

KIM, S., 'Jesus, Sayings of', in *DPL*, ed. G. F. Hawthorne, R. P. Martin and D. G. Reid (Downers Grove and Leicester: IVP, 1993).

——, *Paul and the New Perspective: Second Thoughts on the Origin of Paul's Gospel* (Grand Rapids: Eerdmans, 2002).

LADD, G. E., *A Theology of the New Testament*, rev. ed., ed. D. A. Hagner (Grand Rapids: Eerdmans, 1993).

LIGHTFOOT, J. B., HARMER, J. R., and HOLMES, M. W. (trans. and ed.), *The Apostolic Fathers*, 2nd ed. (Grand Rapids: Baker, 1989).

LONGENECKER, B., *The Triumph of Abraham's God* (Edinburgh: T. & T. Clark, 1998).

LONGENECKER, R. N., *Paul, Apostle of Liberty* (New York: Harper & Row, 1964).

LUTHER, M., 'A Brief Instruction on what to Look for and Expect in the Gospels', in *Luther's Works*, ed. J. Pelikan and H. T. Lehmann, 55 vols. (St. Louis: Concordia; Fortress: Philadelphia, 1955–86).

McGOWAN, A. T. B., 'The Atonement as Penal Substitution', in *Always Reforming: Explorations in Systematic Theology*, ed. A. T. B. McGowan (Leicester: Apollos, 2006), pp. 183–210.

McKNIGHT, S., *Galatians*, NIVAC (Grand Rapids: Zondervan, 1995).

——, *Jesus and His Death: Historiography, the Historical Jesus, and Atonement Theory* (Waco: Baylor University Press, 2005).

MARSHALL, I. H., *1 and 2 Thessalonians*, NCB (Grand Rapids: Eerdmans, 1983).

——, *New Testament Theology: One Gospel, Many Witnesses* (Downers Grove: IVP; Leicester: Apollos, 2004).

MARTIN, R. P., *2 Corinthians*, WBC (Waco: Word, 1986).

——, *Reconciliation: A Study of Paul's Theology* (Atlanta: Westminster John Knox, 1981).

MONTEFIORE, C. G., *Judaism and St. Paul: Two Essays* (London: Macmillan, 1914).

MOO, D. J., *The Epistle to the Romans*, NICNT (Grand Rapids: Eerdmans, 1996).

MORRIS, L., *The Apostolic Preaching of the Cross*, 3rd ed. (Grand Rapids: Eerdmans, 1984).

MURPHY-O'CONNOR, J., *Paul: A Critical Life* (Oxford: Oxford University Press, 1997).

NEUSNER, J., *Genesis Rabbah* (Atlanta: Scholars, 1987).

PACKER, J. I., 'What Did the Cross Achieve? The Logic of Penal

Substitution', *TynBul* 25 (1974), pp. 3–45.

PHILO, trans. C. E. Yonge, *The Complete Works of Philo* (Peabody: Hendrickson, 1993).

PLEVNIK, J., 'The Center of Paul's Theology', *CBQ* 51 (1989), pp. 460–478.

PORTER, S. E., 'Images of Christ in Paul's letters', in *Images of Christ: Ancient and Modern*, ed. S. E. Porter, M. A. Hayes and D. Tombs (Sheffield: Sheffield Academic Press, 1997), pp. 95–112.

——, Katalassō *in Ancient Greek Literature, with Reference to the Pauline Writings* (Cordoba: Ediciónes El Almendro, 1994).

PRICE, S. R. F., *Rituals and Power: The Roman Imperial Cult in Asia Minor* (Cambridge: Cambridge University Press, 1984).

RAMSAY, W. M., *St. Paul the Traveller and Roman Citizen*, 11th ed. (London: Hodder & Stoughton, 1895).

REASONER, M., *Romans in Full Circle: A History of Interpretation* (Louisville: Westminster John Knox, 2005).

RIDDERBOS, H., *Paul: An Outline of His Theology* (Grand Rapids: Eerdmans, 1975).

RIESNER, R., *Paul's Early Period: Chronology, Mission Strategy, Theology*, trans. D. Scott (Grand Rapids: Eerdmans, 1998).

ROBERTS, A., and DONALDSON, J. (eds.), *The Ante-Nicene Fathers*, 10 vols. (Grand Rapids: Eerdmans, 1979 [1885]).

SCHLARB, E., *Die gesunder Lehre: Häeresie und Wahrheit im Spiegel der Pastoralbriefe* (Marburg: N. G. Elwert, 1990).

SCHREINER, T. R., *Paul: Apostle of God's Glory in Christ: A Pauline Theology* (Leicester: Apollos, 2001).

——, 'Penal Substitution View', in *The Nature of the Atonement: Four Views*, ed. P. R. Eddy and J. K. Beilby (Downers Grove: IVP, 2006), pp. 67–98.

SCHWEITZER, A., *Mysticism of Paul the Apostle*, trans. W. Montgomery (Baltimore: Johns Hopkins University Press, 1998 [1931]).

SEGAL, A. F., *Paul the Convert: The Apostolate and Apostasy of Saul the Pharisee* (New Haven: Yale University Press, 1990).

SEIFRID, M., *Christ, our Righteousness*, NSBT 9 (Leicester: Apollos; Downers Grove: IVP, 2000).

STOTT, J., *The Cross of Christ*, rev. ed. (Leicester: IVP, 1989).

STRELAN, R., *Paul, Artemis, and the Jews in Ephesus*, BZNW 80 (Berlin: W. de Gruyter, 1996).

TALBERT, C. H., *Romans* (Macon: Smyth & Helwys, 2002).

THIELMAN, F., *Paul and the Law: A Contextual Approach* (Downers Grove:

IVP, 1994).

THISELTON, A. C., *The First Epistle to the Corinthians*, NIGTC (Grand Rapids: Eerdmans, 2000).

TIDBALL, D., *Skilful Shepherds: Explorations in Pastoral Theology* (Leicester: Apollos, 1997).

TOBIN, T. H., *Paul's Rhetoric in Its Contexts: The Argument of Romans* (Peabody: Hendrickson, 2004).

TOWNER, P. H., *The Letters of Timothy and Titus*, NICNT (Grand Rapids: Eerdmans, 2006).

VICKERS, B., *Jesus' Blood and Righteousness: Paul's Theology of Imputation* (Wheaton: Crossway, 2006).

WALLACE, D. B., *Greek Grammar Beyond the Basics* (Grand Rapids: Zondervan, 1996).

WATSON, F. B., 'The Triune Divine Identity', *JSNT* 80 (2000), pp. 99–124.

WEBSTER, J., *Confessing God: Essays in Christian Dogmatics II* (London: T. & T. Clark, 2005).

WENHAM, D., *Paul: Follower of Jesus or Founder of Christianity?* (Grand Rapids: Eerdmans, 1995).

WITHERINGTON, B., III, *1 and 2 Thessalonians: A Socio-Rhetorical Commentary* (Grand Rapids: Eerdmans, 2006).

——, *Letters and Homilies for Hellenized Christians*, vol. 1: *A Socio-Rhetorical Commentary on Titus, 1–2 Timothy and 1–3 John* (Nottingham: Apollos, 2006).

——, *Paul's Narrative Thought World* (Louisville: Westminster John Knox, 1994).

WRIGHT, N. T., *The Climax of the Covenant* (Edinburgh: T. & T. Clark, 1991).

——, *Paul: Fresh Perspectives* (London: SPCK, 2005).

——, 'Paul's Gospel and Caesar's Empire', <http://www.ctinquiry.org/publications/wright.htm> accessed 4 April 2007.

——, 'The Paul of History and the Apostle of Faith', *TynBul* 29 (1978), pp. 61–88.

——, 'Romans', in *New Interpreters Bible*, ed. L. E. Keck, 12 vols. (Abingdon: Nashville, 2002), vol. 10, pp. 392–770.

——, *What Saint Paul Really Said* (Oxford: Lion, 1997).

INDEX OF NAMES

INDEX OF BIBLICAL REFERENCES

INDEX OF ANCIENT SOURCES